W9-DJH-538

LOOKING INTO HOUSES

LOOKING INTO HOUSES

60 SOLUTIONS TO DESIGN PROBLEMS

BY JAMES BRETT

WHITNEY LIBRARY OF DESIGN
an imprint of
Watson-Guptill Publications / New York, N.Y.

Copyright © 1976 by Whitney Library of Design
First published 1976 in New York by Whitney Library of Design,
an imprint of Watson-Guptill Publications,
a division of Billboard Publications, Inc.,
1515 Broadway, New York, N.Y. 10036

All rights reserved. No part of this publication
may be reproduced or used in any form or by any means—graphic,
electronic, or mechanical, including photocopying, recording, taping,
or information storage and retrieval systems—without
written permission of the publisher.

Library of Congress Cataloging in Publication Data

Brett, James, 1927–
    Looking into houses.
    Includes index.
    1. Photography—Interiors.   2.   Architecture, Domestic—
Designs and plans.   I.   Title.
TR620.B7   779'.4'0924   76-25123
ISBN 0-8230-7358-0

First Printing, 1976

Manufactured in U.S.A.

Acknowledgments

I would like to extend special gratitude to Ben Schnall, one of America's pioneer architectural photographers, whose great good humor, guidance, and understanding gave me the courage to embark on a new career. I would also like to thank Susan Braybrooke and Susan Davis for their editorial assistance during the development of the book. And finally, I am grateful to my wife, Corty, whose patience and companionship made the whole thing possible.

Recognition is due to *The House & Garden Guides*, Condé Nast Publications, Inc.; *New Homes Guide* and *Home Modernizing*, Holt, Rinehart and Winston, Inc.; and *House Beautiful's Special Publications*, Division of the Hearst Corporation, for their cooperation in the use of my photography for this book.

Contents

Preface

As an editor who has published many of James Brett's architectural photographs, I have been looking into houses through Jim Brett's camera for a long time.

Jim Brett represents a relatively new and increasingly vital force in architecture: the architectural photographer. With no particular vested interest, except a love of good design and an appreciation of the architect's role in building a better world, architectural photographers have become an important link between design professionals and the general public.

Most of the view we have of current architecture and design has been filtered through their lenses. Much of the looking into houses that we do would be impossible without them.

What I appreciate about Jim Brett's work, in particular, is his uncanny eye for spotting—then capturing on film—innovative solutions to the typical design problems people resolve with their architects when adding on to, remodeling, or building a new house.

One of my major concerns as a "shelter" editor right now is the shrinking number of Americans who can still afford to realize the American dream of having a special place of their own. That number can grow with a broader view of the architectural design possibilities available, the talent inherent in the architectural profession, and the new ways that houses can be, in fact are being, designed today.

The publication of residential architecture has been one of the most powerful disseminators of modern design ideas and techniques. And as land and building costs continue to rise, new ideas and techniques for building become more important than ever.

Admittedly cost isn't usually the prime factor in what most of us choose to show our readers. I don't think it should be. We're essentially in the idea business, and ideas cannot be limited by price tags.

Brett's chapter on one-room houses, showing how large-scale space is possible in a modest house, is a good example, however, of how ideas do spread. Those one-room houses are the outgrowth of a whole new point of view about what is required or desirable in a house. That point of view was first articulated by architectural greats like Philip Johnson and Marcel Breuer who designed houses where living spaces were conceived as total landscapes, undivided by unnecessary walls and partitions.

When first shown, they were part of very special, often expensive, pace-setting houses. But had they not been shown then because of their price, the public never would have been exposed to their trend-setting ideas, nor would the public have come to accept those ideas as they became part of the design vocabulary of the more modest houses that were to follow. The aesthetic of openness, in fact, became an economical solution in subsequent interpretations.

But new ideas—such as kitchens designed as open elements in living landscapes—have to be well executed in their beginnings by professionals with authority and acknowledged expertise. And then ideas have to be communicated to the public so they can get used to them. Only then can most of us come to understand them, relate to them, and incorporate them as possibilities in our own lives.

Looking into Houses is also a way of looking at how life itself is changing. Juxtaposed with the one-room houses in this book are home hideaways designed for privacy and quiet. Along with brownstone remodelings in New York City, there are remodeled barns in the country. And in addition to lush environments for indoor pools, there are simple, low-cost interior refurbishing ideas.

There are photographs of new houses and houses that have been added onto again and again. There are rooms illustrating the phenomenal growth of interest in plants, the love of country kitchens, and the growing need for places in which to work at home.

The projects themselves best illustrate the reason why communication between design professionals and the public is important. A good idea is a valuable thing—worth hanging onto—and sharing. And that is what Jim Brett is doing here.

Louis Oliver Gropp,
Editor-in-Chief
The House & Garden Guides

Introduction

Twenty years of writing, editing, and photographing for America's shelter magazines have given me a privileged view inside thousands of houses. I have drawn together photographs for this book that I think express the highlights of this experience. The intention of the book is really two-fold. The first is to convey photographically the unique, imaginative, and highly personal solutions of architects and designers to the problems and challenges of creating spaces for living. The second is to share the methods I employ as a photographer for getting this architectural or design statement on film.

The houses I have chosen to include in this book are predominantly economical ones. They are inspired designs developed within the practical limitations of client needs, budget, and site restrictions. They represent imaginative and original solutions to difficult but typical problems the client, architect, and designer face. How each professional has worked with site, climate, orientation, space, mass, form, line, light, texture, and color—all elements inherent in the creation of new living space—determines the distinctive design solution of each project.

In photographing these houses, I have tried to capture the detail, spirit, and entirety of the architect's vision. Rather than simply presenting an accumulation of houses, each chapter here deals with a design theme. These themes, basically architectural, embrace a diversity of ideas that involve the enhancement of the human experience at home. Innovation in and refinement of the specific design exercise were the criteria for the selection of the photographic illustrations. Also, I wanted to cut across design schemes to include specialized areas of living space such as the crow's nests, country kitchens, artists' studios at home, and the increasingly popular green rooms and indoor swimming pools, more and more becoming a part of contemporary home experience, even within budget constraints.

The Designer and the Client

Looking into houses and seeing firsthand the residential work of architects and interior designers has left me with some distinct impressions about the relationship between the architect and his client as it bears on the attainment of a successful project. It is the opinion of many architects with whom I have worked—and my own experience also bears this out—that the ideal climate for a successful design begins with a client who has a point of view about his environment. However, achieving a house that evokes a singular quality—always the most compelling to us and satisfying to the client—is rarely accomplished without the professional who can apply his imagination, intelligence, and discipline in turning an ideal into an actuality.

The client, once he has conveyed his needs and ideas, must be willing to suspend control and allow the architect or designer to express his insight, artistry, and technical facility in his own design language. If this is done, the design solution will very often transcend the goals that the client had thought possible within the limitations of site and budget. Thus the interplay of the client with a point of view and an architect with vision and convictions can lead to a design that is fulfilling to the professional and provides the owner with a quality of shelter that far exceeds his expectations.

I can remember on numerous occasions, as an editor, receiving glowing reports of an owner-executed design project that was "really different." However, on receipt of snapshots or an actual visit to the site, I found that what were good ideas and intentions had run amok and evolved into a reality of utter chaos. Obviously these houses needed the vision and guiding hand of a professional to unify these ideas into an organic whole. To accomplish this, especially with a client who states, "I don't know anything about architecture but I know what I like," often requires patience, dedication, and a knowledge of human nature on the part of the architect to explain his ideas and reasons for them to the client. But I have seen it work with highly gratifying results, not only to the benefit of the design project but to the education and conversion of the client.

I also place great faith in the value of intuition and first impression in design because I have seen these work so many times. After a few hours of discussion with the client and a visit to the site, the architect has been able to sit down and, in a matter of minutes, create a rough pencil sketch of the entire project that proved to be the best solution possible. This instinctive conception withstood countless hours of questioning and indecision on the part of the client.

The Designer and the Editor

Many architects and designers eschew the role of businessman-publicist and effectively keep their work under wraps, almost always to their own detriment. Meanwhile, the supertalents and the more aggressive publish regularly. The most common reason given for not attempting to publicize is lack of time. However, two other aspects also work against the architect: reluctance to risk possible rejection by an editor, combined with a lack of knowledge about how one actually gets a finished project to an editor's desk.

An architect should bear in mind that if he can provide an editor with a good idea or ready-made article, he is doing him a favor and making his job easier. Thus rejection of an architect's or designer's work is much less likely if a well-thought-out idea is proposed to an editor. As for actually getting material to an editor, this is easily accomplished by calling or writing the appropriate editor on a periodical that covers the type of work done by the architect. Most libraries have directories of periodicals that list technical, professional, and consumer publications. These can be scanned for appropriate publications. Also, a perusal of the magazine's masthead will reveal the names of various department editors who can be contacted directly.

An editor will usually require photographs and a brief written description of a finished project. If possible, a visit to the editor with material in hand is preferable to communication only through mail. Also, some magazines will want to photograph the project themselves, while others will require that the designer supply the finished photography. A few publishers may request exclusivity, others first-time rights, while others will place no restrictions on how an architect uses his photography.

Other outlets for publicity include national and local newspapers and manufacturers' brochures and advertisements. Newspaper exposure has proved to be a very effective publicity outlet for many designers. Also, a national magazine article on a designer's work is often in itself a newsworthy item for a local newspaper. If the work highlights a particular manufacturer's product or material, the company may be interested in featuring photographs in its promotional literature or ads and will often give a credit line beside the photograph.

To make the best use of time spent publicizing work, media should be chosen whose readership most nearly coincides with the market an architect or designer wants to reach. Then the editors should be contacted regularly. It has often been the case that when an architect's work has been published a number of times, it is not unusual for editors to begin calling him to keep up with his work.

The Designer-Photographer

The job of the photographer photographing houses is to edit the house pictorially, to catch the views most evocative of the intent of the architect or designer working with three dimensional space. He has to decide what to leave in and what to omit. This requires foreknowledge of what the architect was trying to do and the vision to capture the major strokes of the design in individual pictures.

The architect or interior designer who photographs his own work with a high degree of competency can permanently record and show his work at will. There are several different levels of photographic proficiency that he can aspire to, depending on how much time and expense he can invest in learning the craft and obtaining the proper photographic equipment.

At the primary stage, many designers, using very basic equipment, regularly take "before," "progress," and "after" pictures of every project for their own reference as well as for use in preparing working drawings, checking dimensions and locations, and as evidence against possible lawsuits. "Before" and "progress" pictures can also be included in articles for publication.

Preparation of job file photos takes very little experience or investment in equipment, and a Polaroid camera is adequate in most instances. But if it is necessary to incorporate large areas in one picture, a 35mm camera that accepts interchangeable lenses is necessary. A 28mm wide-angle lens will take in a lot of territory and will be especially useful for indoor views. A light meter, either built in the camera or hand-held, will give an accurate exposure using a fast black-and-white film. If the photographer is working in poorly lighted interior areas, the film can be "pushed" to double or triple its ASA speed. However, the processor must be informed of the speed at which the film was exposed. Also the whole roll of film must be exposed at the same ASA. If a photographic situation requires long exposures because of low light, the camera should be supported on a tripod or on something solid. This would apply to any exposure longer than 1/25 of a second. Or flash illumination may be used. Rechargeable electronic flash units allow exposure setting directly from a dial that is part of the flash unit. Some new models adjust light output automatically.

A mid level of proficiency involves the use of photography for client presentations, business meetings, and trade convention slide shows. Pictures intended for presentation to prospective clients and business associates require clarity of subject matter as the main concern. This type of picture or color slide should be a reasonable record of the architect's work and yet not demand a great expenditure of time, money, and preparation for the photography. The 35mm camera with interchangeable lenses is still the most convenient and adaptable for this purpose, although larger hand-held cameras such as the 2¼″ square format and the 2¼″ x 2¾″ film size will give better resolution in enlargements when prints are made to an 8″ x 10″ size and larger.

In photographing architecture and interiors, the single most important tool is the wide-angle lens. It is impossible, in most cases, to get a comprehensive view either inside or outside without it. Filters also come into play at this stage. For exterior black and whites, a yellow or orange filter is necessary to cut down haze, darken blue skies, and whiten clouds. Since these filters reduce the amount of light that reaches the film, the light meter must be adjusted to the factor of the filter. For color slides outdoors, a haze filter is recommended and does not require an adjustment of exposure.

Depth of field is an important consideration in architectural photography—keeping everything in focus from near the camera to the farthest point of the subject. This can be accomplished by using the smallest aperture possible compatible with the speed selected for the exposure. The slower the shutter speed, the smaller the lens opening. As a general rule, no opening larger than f/11 should be used. Of course, through the use of a tripod, much longer exposures can be made, and the lens can be shut down to f/22 or f/32 to bring almost everything into sharp focus.

The tripod is also useful in helping keep the camera straight vertically and horizontally. This is particularly important in photographing buildings to insure that the vertical lines of the structure are kept parallel in the picture. This can be checked through the view finder and also by using a liquid level on the body of the camera.

At this point the developing and printing of photographs may need reconsideration if the photographer has been having them sent out and processed on a mass production basis. It is strongly suggested that a custom laboratory be found that can be dealt with on a personal basis so the kind of finished prints that suit the architect's needs can be realized. In the developing and printing, the lab technician can correct some of the errors made in exposure.

The highest or professional level of photography is aimed for publication, design competitions, and public display. If the photographs are intended for general distribution, the architect should be prepared to assimilate a second vocation into his life. Photographing professionally is essentially an all-or-nothing undertaking. It is either done consistently and well or infrequently and with mediocre results. While it is not possible to cover all the technical aspects of a refined picture-taking process, the major preoccupations and considerations will be touched on here.

While adequate results can sometimes be obtained with hand-held cameras, the standard and accepted camera is the 4" x 5" view camera mounted on a tripod. A few photographers still use the big 8" x 10" camera as standard equipment. The large negative size of these cameras permits enlargements that are sharp and clear even when blown up to giant display sizes. The lens and film planes are adjustable so architectural subjects can be rendered fully and with minimum distortion. The lenses are interchangeable, and a strong tripod is always needed. Lights, stands, and electrical leads are essential for most interior shots. Other items to be included in a typical basic outfit would be a light meter, filters for black-and-white and color films, holders for sheet film, packs of 16-sheet black-and-white film, and normal wide-angle and extreme wide-angle lenses.

It will take time to get used to working with large and varied equipment; this can be done only by actually going through the steps of photographing a variety of architectural subjects. For a good technical guide to the use of the 4" x 5" camera, *Photography with Large-Format Cameras*, published by Eastman Kodak Company, is recommended reading.

Photographing design work requires an analysis of the project itself, whether the subject is the redecoration of one room or the design of an entire building. Some questions that should be asked in the process are: Why is the job important? What aspects are to be emphasized, underplayed, or omitted from the photography? From what viewpoints are the design elements best seen? How will the subject be broken down into individual views? What angle gives the most comprehensive view of the subject? At what times of day do the different areas look best in relation to the sun?

The designer of the scene to be photographed will have definite ideas about the high points of the design and the angles from which the subject looks best and is most comprehensible. It's also useful to walk through the project and list the views to be included and the order in which they are to be photographed, keeping in mind the position of the sun and the ease of transition from one location to another. This advance preparation provides one with a mental note of things that have to be moved or changed and the accessories or furnishings that must be added or deleted.

Each scene is viewed through the ground glass, since that is how the camera records the picture—not as it is seen with the naked eye. The concept of each picture should be as clear and simple as possible, with no extraneous or distracting elements included.

There are numerous considerations for the viewing and editing of each scene. Is too much or too little being included in the composition? The composition should be tight and cogent. Does the subject matter make more sense as a vertical or horizontal composition? Verticals usually have a stronger composition and are more suitable to publication format. Where is the best position for the lights? It's best to avoid double shadows, dark spots, hot spots, glare, and reflections from windows and mirrors. What is the best height for the camera? Overlapping objects because of low camera position should be avoided, but a too high elevation looks unnatural. Is there too much ceiling in the picture? The lens can be lowered, or it can be raised if there is too much floor. Are the windows and shades at different heights? They should be even and uniform.

Another consideration is how the photographs will be used. In photographing for one or more possible magazine showings, 8″ x 10″ black-and-white prints may be all that are necessary. However color transparencies may be required. If color prints are to be made, taking negative color can save the cost of making an internegative. In cases where color slides are called for, the 35mm camera will be used.

When interiors are photographed in color, the type of lighting used must agree with the film type. Type B Ektachrome and negative "L" color call for a 3200 degree Kelvin light source, whether it is floodlamp or quartz light. Mixing incandescent light with daylight or fluorescent light can create bizarre colors.

These notes on photographing houses are not meant to be highly technical or inclusive. It is hoped that they will be useful to the architect or designer who desires information on how to take his own photographs. My experience of working with architects, interior designers, and homeowners as both an editor and photographer has been invigorating and instructive. The dedication, technical expertise, and imagination that America's designers have invested in our homes have made them without equal anywhere in the world. It is my hope that the examples of their work shown here will help to inspire the continuation of a great tradition of professionalism in the creation of new homes and the improvement and restoration of the old.

1. One-Room Houses

Each house in this section is comprised of essentially one huge room, but these definitely are not houses of the one-room schoolhouse genre. Each is an architectural tour de force dramatically accomplished within the limits of residential design.

 Each architect aimed to create one grand space, a sculptured volume that would seem to fairly burst the limits of the structure. While some may feel the scale to be dehumanizing, my experience on entering these houses was one of wonder, excitement, and awe that the architect accomplished what he did in what appears from the outside to be a modest domicile. Having experienced these three designs convinced me permanently that looking into houses is a pursuit that holds infinite possibilities.

A Wedge in Wood

Acutely angled and wood sheathed, this diminutive one-space house sits beautifully on its wooded and rocky site in Westchester County, New York. The complete shape of the structure is immediately visible from within and without. Three broad bands of glass illuminate the interior from front and back, and a triangular slice of glass intersects one side wall from the roof to the floor. Punctuating the interior space is a brick slab that houses the fireplace on the living room side, forms one wall of the kitchen to the rear, and, on the second floor, partitions two bedrooms from the living room.

 The living room of this house (opposite), with its contrast and interplay of richly patterned woods, textured brick masonry, and sunlit glass, offers a sensual architectural experience. Sharply angled planes of roof and walls emphasize the strength of the structure. The seemingly endless space of the living room is exaggerated by the vanishing perspective of the receding lines of the ceiling boards. The four cubicles arranged on two levels beyond the brick wall provide a contrast in space. The house is owned by Mr. and Mrs. Gene Robins. Davis, Brody & Associates, Architects.

Photography note. The single most important shot of this house is the overall interior view shown here, since it expresses the theme of the house and the central concept of the architect. A corner aspect from the low end of the living room was chosen to show the rising roof line, the living room space in the foreground, the masonry pier, and the two-story areas beyond. The plane of the film had to be perfectly vertical to keep all the vertical lines in the picture parallel.

Above. The view from the parking area shows the unusual shape of the house. The front and rear walls are actually planes of the roof, while the side walls form scalene triangles.

Right. The raised position of the house not only eliminates some of the problems created by an uneven site but also provides a panoramic view over the surrounding wooded area.

Above. Two flights and a landing comprise the open-railinged, decorative staircase that leads to the second-floor bedroom balcony. A music corner fits in the space between the stairs and the sliding glass doors that open to the rear deck.

Left. The rising plane of the roof draws the eye upward from all parts of the living room, while the bedroom balcony affords an opposite view from which the living room is seen in a plan perspective. A house-wide wall of sliding glass extends the living space outdoors.

Below. A large wall of sliding glass opens the living room to a rear deck that almost doubles the available living space in warm weather. The slanting house walls continue along the sides of the deck to shield the area for privacy and to block winds. The high elevation of the deck above the sloping ground below puts the sitting area in the treetops. The rear railing also provides built-in seating.

Opposite page. The master bedroom on second-floor balcony overlooks the living room and is a part of the single continuum of space. The bold plane of the ceiling flows unbroken from the lowest to the highest house walls. A massive slab of brick nominally defines the bedroom area.

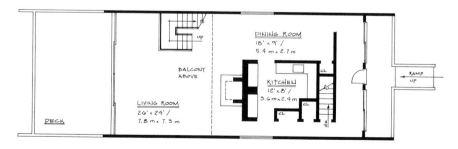

DINING ROOM
18' x 9' /
5.4 m x 2.7 m

BALCONY ABOVE

LIVING ROOM
26' x 24' /
7.8 m x 7.3 m

KITCHEN
12' x 8' /
3.6 m x 2.4 m

RAMP
UP

UP

DECK

FIRST FLOOR PLAN

A Country Retreat

A Princeton, New Jersey architect with a busy practice needed a refuge where he could work without interruption. He found the ideal location in the rolling countryside of western New Jersey near the Pennsylvania state line. The design was a potpourri of early English styles. What appears to be a cozy provincial farmhouse from the outside is a cathedral of space inside—one continuous open space with the exception of the timber-and-brick kitchen extension. William M. Thompson, Architect-owner.

Above. A collection of colonial detailing makes up the house exterior: salt-box extension from the gable roof over the kitchen wing; small-paned casement and bay windows; walls clad in clapboard, brick and timber, and barn siding; and the narrow-board front door with iron strap hinges and a strip of small panes above.

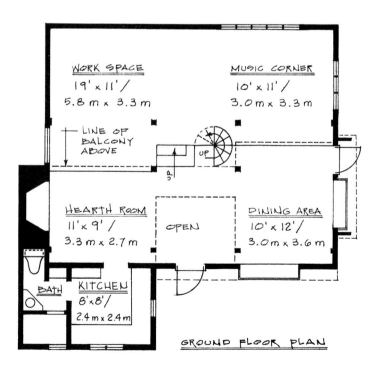

WORK SPACE
19' x 11' /
5.8 m x 3.3 m

MUSIC CORNER
10' x 11' /
3.0 m x 3.3 m

LINE OF BALCONY ABOVE

UP

HEARTH ROOM
11' x 9' /
3.3 m x 2.7 m

OPEN

DINING AREA
10' x 12' /
3.0 m x 3.6 m

BATH

KITCHEN
8' x 8' /
2.4 m x 2.4 m

GROUND FLOOR PLAN

Left. Many of the exposed framing members in the interior were reclaimed from a nearby 150-year-old farmhouse that was torn down. Two main posts support the roof weight, while two shorter posts beyond hold up the balcony. The virtually transparent handmade wooden circular stairs take up minimum space.

Below. The balcony area extends the length of the house and overlooks the living area below. An open well of space divides the two bedrooms on the second level and makes the entry area a roof-high space. Throughout the house, the structure is strongly expressed by the exposure of the framing members—roof rafters, collar beams, and the large posts and beams that support the roof. A formation of birds in flight, executed in thin strips of metal, makes a delicate tracery against the pure white of the chimney breast.

Photography note. The photographic approach to the house was to select one viewpoint that would give the best overall feeling of the interior and then shoot each individual activity area separately. Too many comprehensive angles create confusion and repetition.

Opposite page. The simplicity and order of the interior scheme is carried through even to the architect's work area where the two-story-high north window assures an abundance of constant light. While decorative accessories have been kept to a minimum in the house interior, two interesting items stand out in the work area—the symmetrically arranged organ pipes on a wall-hung shelf and the free-standing metal weather vane next to the drawing table.

Above. The end opposite the work area on the upper level of the main floor contains the sitting-music room. At the right of the sofa a case stores audio components and books, and two leather and brass campaign chairs in the foreground complete the furniture arrangement. The low sloping ceiling and casement windows create a warm, secluded atmosphere. Hanging from the post at right is a bootmaker's dummy.

Below. The hearthroom, as architect Thompson calls it, is neatly tucked into a space three steps below the work area and next to the kitchen wing at left. The large, shallow-arched fireplace, the brick floor, the thick wood joists, and especially the exposed floor boards contribute to the old-world feeling of the room. Here, as throughout the rest of the house, a background of pure white accents the rich wood colors and textures. A long cushion along the ledge provides additional seating.

Glass Shell by the Sound

This one-space house occupies a small site on the Connecticut shore of Long Island Sound. The water view and southern exposure dictated the design of the house as one giant room that would harmonize with the beauty and scale of the horizon view. Caswell Cooke, Architect.

Below. The size of this trim, geometric house conveys the feeling that it would fit easily inside its own living room. The two windowed sides of the house look out over the water while blank walls face the neighbors. Strict alignment of glass openings in the front elevation contrast with the loose organization of side openings, somewhat reminiscent of a Mondrian composition.

Opposite page. The sense of human scale in the living room is completely unlike that felt outside the house. Vertical, horizontal, and slanting planes artfully divide and define the huge open volume. As in the first house in this section, the cross stroke of balcony and a vertical panel behind the fireplace and chimney separate background rooms from the open space.

Above. Looking down at the living room from the mid-level main entry creates the opposite sensation from the living room view on the preceding page— great depth rather than height. The large windows create a particularly strong impact from this vantage point, while the beaded curtains diffuse the light reflected from the water.

Right. The lowest level of the house contains the kitchen and dining area, with the fireplace and its vertical panel separating them from the living room. A light well over the rear wall of the kitchen bathes this seemingly remote area in sunlight, and the open shelves make utensils easy to find.

Left. From the parking area the Sound is seen in the background, and the kitchen extension at left reveals a large glass window well. A fin wall, in front, shields the stairway that leads to the entry level above the living room.

Below. At the mid-level entry to the house, stairs rise to the top floor comprised of two bedrooms and a bath. A bed-sofa under the stairs is an ideal quiet spot for reading or adequate for the accommodation of an overnight guest.

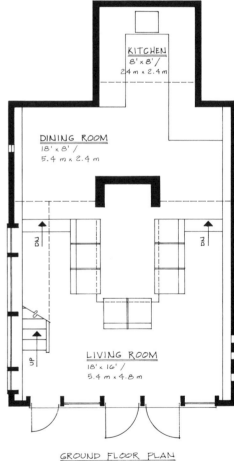

KITCHEN
8' × 8' /
2.4 m × 2.4 m

DINING ROOM
18' × 8' /
5.4 m × 2.4 m

DN   DN

UP

LIVING ROOM
18' × 16' /
5.4 m × 4.8 m

GROUND FLOOR PLAN

Photography note. The tight organization of spaces in this house make a strong composition: bold architectural shapes are graphically arresting and the variety of volumes give depth to the picture. An extreme wide-angle lens was necessary to photograph the interiors because there was little floor space in relation to the great ceiling heights. Also, only a wide angle of view could capture the expansiveness of the big room.

2.Compacts

Putting together the small house is an exacting exercise for the architect and one in which he takes delight and satisfaction. The demands of economy in budget and space require design solutions that are clear, direct, and spare. Here, "less is more" definitely applies.

While being spartan, the architect must be a magician, too—a wizard in creating the illusion of space—using transparency, small scale, continuous lines of sight, and unbroken planes of materials to achieve a harmony of parts that make the house a totality.

Apart from the esthetic satisfactions of designing a complete house in minimum space, functional advantages also exist: low cost of construction, furnishing, maintenance, and operation; adaptability to small and difficult sites; and ease and convenience of use.

Small House in the Woods

Like an intricately faceted gem, the parts of this Putnam County, New York house fit together with exquisite exactness. The plan is laid out in a cruciform shape with all the activity areas directly accessible from the entry axis. The interiors have great spatial variety, with refreshing contrast between solid and transparent planes. Structure and materials are expressed with strength and harmony, and the use of earth-colored bricks and natural-finished wood achieves an organic unity between design, materials, and site. Frank Edward Dushin, Architect.

The living room (opposite) borrows space from the center core of the house. The architect employed every ingenuity to create openness: space flows up and down between levels, opens out from the low-ceilinged dining area to roof height over the living room, and is accentuated by the glass door, a vertical glass strip, and the uninterrupted materials in the background.

Photography note. The exterior views presented photographic difficulties because of the deep shadows around the house from overhangs and tall trees. Also, the dark exterior walls of the house were of the same value as the earth and wood tones. Many interiors required the use of an extreme wide-angle lens to include the high ceilings and interconnecting areas in the foreground. The architectural nature of the furnishings made little rearrangement necessary.

Opposite page. The dining area on entry level overlooks the living room. When not in use, the table retracts to the wall to open space. Skylights illuminate interior space.

Right. This kitchen is an efficient step-saver, with a T-window to bring in light despite the heavily wooded site. A cross bar of glass opens the view uphill, while roof-high ceilings repeatedly achieve additional space.

Right. In the playroom seen from the entry hall, full carpeting provides plenty of sit-down play area for youngsters. Roof-high ceiling and glass walls contribute to the illusion of space. Bunkrooms are at left, with circular stairs leading to a second-story guest-room-den planned for the future. Stairs at the end of the deck in the background lead to grounds outside so children can go in and out without disturbing the rest of the house.

Below left. Bunkrooms are small with built-in and raised sleeping and storage units that facilitate easy cleaning and provide an illusion of wall-to-wall space. Doors slide on tracks set in an exposed ceiling beam.

Below right. The deck off the playroom provides outdoor activity space for children—one wing of the house is theirs: bunkrooms, playroom, and deck. Zoning gives them the privacy and freedom they need and helps keep the rest of the house quiet.

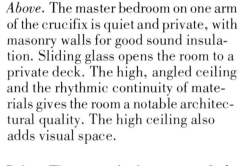

Above. The master bedroom on one arm of the crucifix is quiet and private, with masonry walls for good sound insulation. Sliding glass opens the room to a private deck. The high, angled ceiling and the rhythmic continuity of materials gives the room a notable architectural quality. The high ceiling also adds visual space.

Below. The master bath conveys a feeling of luxury because the architect sustained his design theme through to the smallest details: wall and ceiling planes are boldly expressed and without interruption, and tiny counter tiles are fixed to backing sheets and grouted in place.

Beginner's House

This small rectangle of wood-shingled space was designed for a young family in Westchester County, New York who did not require a larger, more costly house. The interior arrangement of space is an expert adaptation to the requirements of the simple shape of the low-cost structure. An enclosed space of only 1,147 square feet/103.2 square meters is divided into clearly defined areas of use: living, working, sleeping. An entry foyer that opens to the bedroom zone keeps all unnecessary traffic from this quiet area. The open-planned living-dining room with walls of glass provides a public area, while the kitchen utility space is somewhat autonomous with its own outside entrance.

For all its pared-down efficiency, the house has warmth and personality resulting from the architect's deft handling of the materials and structural details. Iver Lofving, Architect.

Above. Three banks of sliding doors 10′/3m wide comprise the exterior bedroom wall of the house. The depth of the house was designed to fit this module, and extensive glass on two opposite walls of the house provides light, space, and view for the interiors. A future deck can further expand these rooms.

Photography note. Despite the smallness of the house, only two views presented any difficulty in finding an acceptable camera position. The overall picture of the living room was taken from outside the house and from a low camera level to accent the volume of the space rather than the furnishings. The exterior view of the bedroom side of the house had to be taken with an extreme wide-angle lens to get the two house walls in the picture without including many trees in the foreground.

Above left. The entrance hall opens to front deck through sliding glass doors, with the living room in the background. The hallway to the bedrooms is at the left of the camera. Redwood decoratively enhances the entry: jointed tongue-and-groove boards on the wall at left and laid open-spaced on the ceiling. A child's swing chair and potted plants hang from the deck beams.

Above right. Addition of the entry deck complete with ample seating space extends the floor plan on to the site. A contemporary treatment of the deck structure suits the house and creates an exterior volume that is room-like, enhanced by the trellised roof which casts changing shadow patterns through the day.

Left. The entry side of the house faces the driveway parking area. A slab-columned front deck was added after the original design was completed. The simplicity of the cube enclosure clad in cedar shingles creates a union between the house and wooded site.

Right. The intimate breakfast room is convenient to the kitchen for informal dining yet out of the way of the kitchen activities. The niche contains storage space for wine and china.

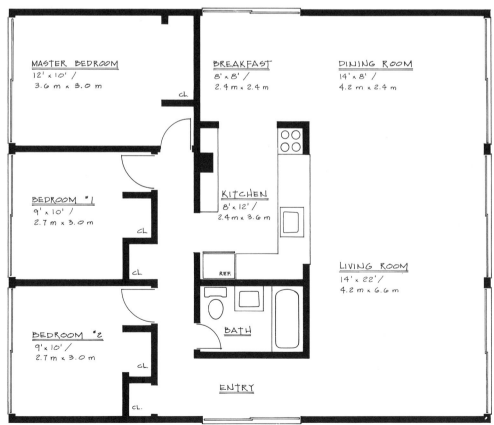

MASTER BEDROOM
12' x 10' /
3.6 m x 3.0 m

BREAKFAST
8' x 8' /
2.4 m x 2.4 m

DINING ROOM
14' x 8' /
4.2 m x 2.4 m

CL.

BEDROOM #1
9' x 10' /
2.7 m x 3.0 m

KITCHEN
8' x 12' /
2.4 m x 3.6 m

CL.

CL.

LIVING ROOM
14' x 22' /
4.2 m x 6.6 m

REF.

BEDROOM #2
9' x 10' /
2.7 m x 3.0 m

BATH

CL.

ENTRY

CL.

FIRST FLOOR PLAN

Above. The living-dining room was planned as one large space to relieve any feeling of confinement in the small house. The pass-through makes the kitchen part of the scene.

Left. Valance lighting in the dining area bathes the walls in light.

Little Liberty Farm

Stepping across the threshold of this Lilliputian house in Connecticut for the first time is like entering another world with everything scaled down to about three-quarters its customary size. However, the family living here has found no problems adjusting to its smallness. They find it so agreeable that they've named it "Little Liberty Farm."

Like many early American houses, the exact origin of this one is unknown. As is often the case, many additions and alterations have been made over the years to fit the needs of a succession of owners. A flat-roofed extension

at the front of the basic two-story structure encloses the entry and dining room. In the rear a shed-roof addition contains the study and a storage closet.

Saving old and historic houses from destruction is of great concern to those who wish to preserve our architectural traditions and maintain a continuity with the past. The most vital kind of conservation is achieved when these fine houses can be perpetuated through occupation by present generations.

Photography note. The extremely limited space in this house made equipment handling difficult—in most cases

only one 1,000-watt lamp would fit into a room. Because most of the camera positions were from the doorways to the rooms, it was necessary to arrange the picture before the camera was set up, since the camera would block the entry. An extreme wide-angle lens was needed for every interior view.

Above. Colonial detailing of the house exterior has been kept intact over the years—narrow-lap clapboard siding; louvered shutters; small-pane, double-hung windows; shed-roof extension at the rear; and a widow's walk over the front entry addition.

Below left. A recessed bay window accents the warm and secluded study at the rear of the house and creates visual space for the room as well as providing couch space for children.

Below right. The long dining table fits the proportions of the dining room and is positioned along the outside wall to allow space for passage between the entry and the living room at right.

Bottom. Box beams in the living room ceiling enclose the original exposed joists. The small-scaled furnishings were chosen to fit precisely into the available space. The body of the fireplace and chimney, when added, was planned to extend outside the house to save floor space inside.

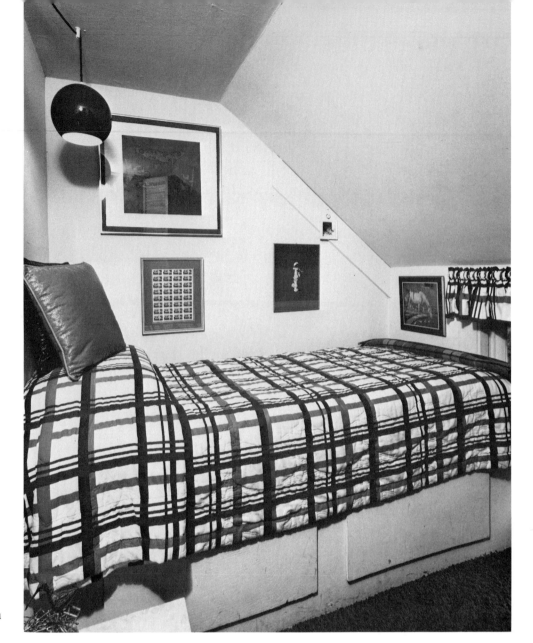

Above. This bedroom is like an efficiently planned sleep capsule. The built-in bunk with storage drawers extends the entire length of the room. A knee-high window provides ventilation but only a limited view.

Below. Despite doorways and a large window that subtract from available wall space, all the necessary kitchen equipment and storage fit into this small room. Even breakfast for two is possible in the space between the oven and the sink.

Above. A delightful free-form swimming pool nests between the house and the wooded property line at the left. Underwater lights and gas-fired torches make the pool a center for warm evening parties. A waterfall pours over a large glacial rock at the far end of the pool recirculating water from the filter system.

Left. Correspondingly small in scale, the garden house echoes the design of the main structure.

Designer–Builder–Owner

A twenty-three-year-old architecture student designed and built his own house on eastern Long Island, New York, with, as he says, "help from my wife, my father-in-law, and a friend." At a construction cost of $14 per square foot/$126 per square meter, this strongly articulated mini-cube is an uncommon example of good design, cost consciousness, and hard work.

Clarity and simplicity of concept are the keynotes to the success and economy of this design. The house is a square, 28′ x 28′/8.6m x 8.6m, with a total of 1,568 square feet/141.1 square meters on two floors. The regular, uncomplicated shape of the house, the extensive use of a few, inexpensive materials, and the concentration of water supply and waste systems cut costs of labor and materials. The fact that the owner was his own architect and builder also helped make this exceptional feat possible.

Locating the living area of the house on the second floor gave a view and openness to the most used areas. Although well planted with young trees, the flat and sandy site offered no great advantage as an extension of the inside living area. Thus the deck off the living room conveniently accommodates outdoor living. The surprising variety in the interior space is accomplished by the open planning of the second floor and the two-story height of the skylighted entry and stairwell. William F. White, Designer-builder.

Photography note. Open-planned interiors can often be difficult to photograph, since the sequence of picture compositions must be framed entirely by the camera with no help from structural partitions. But in this house, the spaces were so well proportioned and related that they defined themselves. Some movement of the furnishings and accessories was needed to fill void spaces in the foregrounds.

Above. A deck projects from the second-story living room at the rear of the house. Almost all the windows located at the corners break into the rectangular shape and provide a sweeping view of the surrounding woodlands. Simultaneously simple and sophisticated, this two-story box achieves high esthetic values on a tight budget. Softly weathering knotty cedar siding covers all.

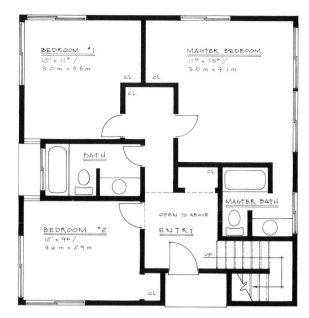

FIRST FLOOR PLAN

BEDROOM #1
10' x 11'6"
3.0 m x 3.5 m

MASTER BEDROOM
11'6" x 13'6"
3.5 m x 4.1 m

CL.

CL.

CL.

BATH

CL

MASTER BATH

OPEN TO ABOVE

BEDROOM #2
12' x 9'6"
3.6 m x 2.9 m

ENTRY

UP

CL.

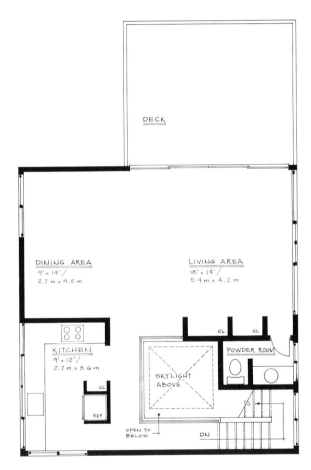

SECOND FLOOR PLAN

DECK

DINING AREA
9' x 14'
2.7 m x 4.2 m

LIVING AREA
18' x 14'
5.4 m x 4.2 m

CL

CL

POWDER ROOM

KITCHEN
9' x 12'
2.7 m x 3.6 m

SKYLIGHT
ABOVE

CL

REF

OPEN TO
BELOW

DN

Above. The two-story-high entry well with roof skylight allows the entire space to be flooded with light. The view from the top of the stairs shows the kitchen at the left and the dining room in the far background.

Below. The entry hall located in the center of the lower level channels traffic directly to the first floor bedrooms and up to the second-story living space. Quarry tile floor cleans easily.

Above. The high strip windows in the living room let in light yet keep the interior entirely private. The decoration and furnishings were kept simple, with the living room furniture arrangement centering around the fireplace.

Right. The living room space expands through the glass wall to the deck. The high windows do not interrupt the flow of the wall space which is excellent for hanging paintings. Note the reverse use of open and solid spaces in the adjoining right-angle walls.

Opposite page. A deeply recessed well housing two skylights separates the dining and kitchen areas. The heavy masses and slanting planes emphasize the strong architectural quality of the space.

Above. The dropped ceiling over the dining area defines it as a distinct space and provides intimacy. The painting on the far wall gives a strong linear perspective to the room when seen from the kitchen, framed on top by the low ceiling and at bottom by the pass-through counter.

Right. In pleasant weather the deck doubles as a second living room, its height keeping it private from the neighbors and giving an excellent overview of the wooded areas nearby.

Island in the Fields

Two-storied and tightly planned, this house stands watch over a flat plain of grass on eastern Long Island, New York. The design is like a Chinese puzzle of precisely interlocking geometric parts. The owner of this weekend house required simplicity, convenience, and originality of design for a small family. Low maintenance, minimal housework, and ease of use are prime objectives when planning a vacation home and are well served here by the simply detailed structure and diminutive and tightly knit spaces. The division of the compact interior into two levels provides quiet and privacy for the bedrooms.

The long vistas across farm land to the south and east initiated the two-level concept that would place the living areas on top, providing access to the horizon-far view. Decks on either side of the living room add to the interior space, make outdoor living convenient, and take full advantage of the elevation. Openness between living, dining, and kitchen areas and the abundant glass add further to the spaciousness of the second floor. Eugene Futterman, Architect.

Above. The approach to the house from the parking area reveals smoothly flowing curves and sharply delineated planes. The farm-derivative silo shape in the foreground encloses the entry and stairwell. A vertical slit window lights the stair column. Cedar shingles adapt well to the curved surfaces of the exterior.

Above. The stairwell in the background rises to the living level. The windows all around provide light, view, and spaciousness.

Right. The railinged deck outside the upper-level living room overlooks an almost endless view of grassy fields.

Photography note. Photographing the exterior of this house was relatively simple, since the house is in the open and square shaped. Care was taken to reveal as much as possible of the curves, angles, and planes of the structure. Despite compact interior space, open planning gave enough room for camera placement so extreme wide-angle lenses were not needed.

Left. Small houses seem to have the most efficient kitchens—everything within arm's reach. The panel of fixed glass over the work counter reveals both the view and the shape of the structure. The dining area is beyond.

Below. The deck on the south side of the house basks in warm sun most of the day. The upstairs living space is expanded on both sides by decks that extend above the bedrooms below. The vantage point from the elevated deck above the flat terrain gives one a sense of being at sea.

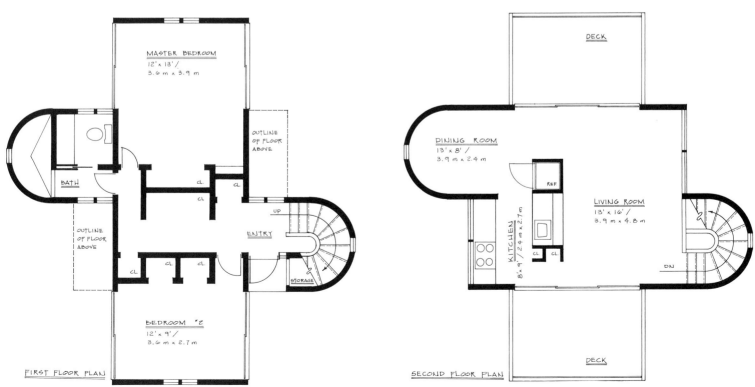

FIRST FLOOR PLAN

MASTER BEDROOM
12' x 13' /
3.6 m x 3.9 m

OUTLINE
OF FLOOR
ABOVE

BATH

OUTLINE
OF FLOOR
ABOVE

CL.

CL.

CL.

CL.

CL.

CL.

UP

ENTRY

STORAGE

BEDROOM #2
12' x 9' /
3.6 m x 2.7 m

SECOND FLOOR PLAN

DECK

DINING ROOM
13' x 8' /
3.9 m x 2.4 m

REF

KITCHEN
8' x 9' / 2.4 m x 2.7 m

CL.

CL.

LIVING ROOM
13' x 16' /
3.9 m x 4.8 m

DN

DECK

Spectacle in Small Space

Acutely angled rooms, a wide array of windows, open loft spaces, and rising roof planes are a few of the surprises held by this small, two-unit house on eastern Long Island, New York. The binuclear plan separates the active and passive living areas into two structures connected by an entry canopy and a common deck plaza. The walls of the house and the rise of the land from the parking area work together to create a subtle drama of withholding a vast ocean view until the deck is reached. Smith and Munter, Architects.

Left. Seen from the arrival point, the two separate masses of the house do not yet reveal the focus of the design. The outer walls of the two house wings shield the interior and the deck from the neighbors and the street.

Opposite page. The entry walkway splits the two house units and thrusts outward beneath the connecting overhang, revealing a hint of the ocean view. Space compressed under the low canopy expands sky-high once the deck is reached.

Photography note. The variety and unfolding of space in this house made the photographic assignment both exciting and demanding. The strength of the design made picture composition easy. Extreme wide-angle lenses were needed to include the great ceiling heights.

DECK

LIVING ROOM
18' x 16' /
5.4 m x 4.8 m

UP

CL. REF.

KITCHEN 12' x 8' /
3.6 m x 2.4 m

BEDROOM
12' x 9' /
3.6 m x 2.7 m

CL. CL.

BEDROOM
12' x 6' /
3.6 m x 1.8 m

BATH

DINING ROOM
13' x 20' /
3.9 m x 6.1 m

UP UTILITY

CL.

FIRST FLOOR PLAN

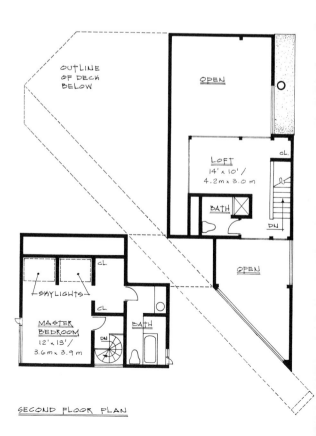

OUTLINE OF DECK BELOW

OPEN

LOFT
14' x 10' /
4.2 m x 3.0 m

CL.

BATH

DN

OPEN

SKYLIGHTS

CL.

CL.

MASTER BEDROOM
12' x 13' /
3.6 m x 3.9 m

BATH

DN

SECOND FLOOR PLAN

Above. Seemingly endless space stretches from the deck to the horizon. What first appeared to be a small house on a tiny, uninteresting site is, in fact, a home with a panorama of the rim of the world.

Right. The deck fits privately into the L-shape of the house whose wings protect the deck on two sides. The large trapezoidal window opens the master bedroom to light and view. The sliding glass doors open the living room to the deck.

Below. An open structure gives much to look at inside. An alleyway leads past the dining area at right, then to the kitchen, and on into the two-story-high dining room.

Below left. The volume of the master bedroom is boldly expressed by the exposed ceiling structure, the geometry of the window, and minimal decoration.

Above right. Another splendid interior view is that of the dining room seen from the top of the stairs. The fan light window over the French doors is an added traditional touch.

Left. The perspective in the acute-angled dining room is exaggerated by the slanting wall boards vanishing in the apex of the trapezoidally shaped room. The high window provides an abundance of light and preserves the privacy of the room from the deck entry. Note the high electric heating units on the wall—they bathe the windows with rising warm air in the cooler months.

3. Townhouses

Creating a private and personal haven in an often faceless city is a tour de force of determination, hard work, good taste, imagination, and money.

While many might be satisfied with the coolness and anonymity of contemporary, luxury, high-rise apartments, others seek an identification with the past when a city such as New York was warmer—a place of closely knit neighborhoods and finely detailed beaux-arts facades, a city where residential buildings were designed on a human scale rather than as great cliffs of concrete and steel.

All five examples of remodeling for city living in this chapter are located in New York City. Four are townhouse renovations and the other is one of 144 apartment-studios built in an abandoned, cast-iron-fronted department store on lower Broadway. In all cases, the architects have created warm and hospitable dwellings while simultaneously saving lovely and venerable buildings from destruction.

Rowhouse Renovation

Built in the 1880's, this five-story brownstone (opposite) had weathered almost a century of use and disuse. It most recently had been a rooming house with an interior of many squalid cubicles. The architect, along with others interested in upgrading the neighborhood bought houses on this west-side street in Manhattan. They wanted to remodel them for their own homes and at the same time set an example for others to follow. The venture has been individually successful and a worthy model for those who built after them. Stephen B. Jacobs, Architect.

Photography note. Photographing the interiors of the townhouse presented a challenge because of the narrowness of the rooms. An extreme wide-angle lens was needed to include the high ceilings and to encompass the relationships between adjacent areas in an open plan.

Above. At the rear of the main living level are the family room, dining area, and kitchen, once a hive of partitions. Removal of old wall coverings reveals the bare brick of the wall and understates the framework of the room. The two-story-high window extending from the family room floor level to the master bedroom above emphasizes vertical space.

Left. The stairway at midpoint on the main level leads to a mezzanine study, while the flight at right rises to the bedroom floor. Valance lighting illuminates the white-painted brick fireplace.

Opposite page. Shuttered windows at the front of the house control light and privacy. This room is used mainly for small-group entertaining.

New Ideas Next Door

When the architect of the previous house finished remodeling his own brownstone, the buyer of the house next door was so impressed that she commissioned him to renovate her building. The two long and narrow structures are almost identical in size—19′ x 68′/5.6m x 20.8m. The problems and solutions were almost the same also; however, the end result is not identical. Each house emerged with a distinctive character of its own.

Photography note. Again, the photographic requirements for this house were similar to its mate next door—to capture in a narrow width the high ceilings and long flow of spaces, using an extreme wide-angle lens. Care was taken to point up differences between the two units.

Opposite page. The front steps and entry porch that led from the sidewalk to the second floor of the house were removed, and the entry vestibule for the six apartments in the building is now at street level. The dining room window, under the central pediment, was the location of the original front door. The section drawing below shows the arrangement of the rooms.

Right. The delicately carved newel post and second-level railing are wood decorations that were originally on the outside of the house. A cut-out niche for a plant at the first landing opens the stairway to a view from the living room.

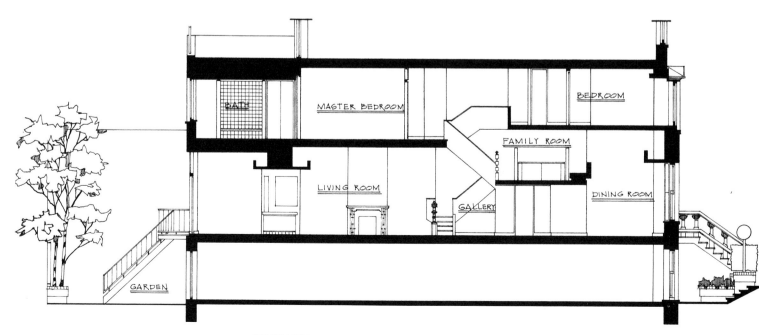

SECTION

Opposite page. A strong sense of vertical space is apparent in the view down the staircase from the highest level bedroom hall. A centered chandelier dramatizes the vertical volume. The original brick is painted white, as are all the walls and ceilings.

Above. The white fireplace wall is brightly lit from the cove above. An ornamental wood fireplace surround is the only decoration left from the original heavily wood-trimmed room. The French doors beyond the bar lead to a rear garden.

Below. An oriental rug, paintings, and a few brightly colored pillows are the only decorative accents used against a passive background emphasizing the most important design element—space.

Opposite page. A highly original and effective lighting treatment is achieved in this workable, galley-style kitchen by recessing jumbo long-life bulbs in coffers between the ceiling joists. The countertop is made of terracotta clay tiles. The high window ensures the privacy of the breakfast room in the background.

Above. Steel crossbeams made possible the suspension of the family room on an intermediate level in the open space between the stairway gallery and the dining room. Open on both ends, the room has a view of the entire length of the house.

Right. A view across the dining room reveals the breakfast room at left, a pass-through to the kitchen for serving, and at top right, the sofa wall of the family room. Space flows freely in all directions from this vantage point.

Refurbished Brownstone

This five-story brownstone was built in the mid-nineteenth century as a one-family house and, as is often the case in the changing city, was sold and turned into small apartment units. It deteriorated over the years until it was bought by a young family. The new owners occupy the two lower levels and rent out the upper stories. The two bottom floors were gutted to accommodate the new floor plan, but the ceilings were left at standard height to provide rooms that would have a "house-like" scale. Working within the railroad-car proportions of a long, narrow building, the architect devised a highly workable floor plan that maintains the privacy of individual rooms. Stephen B. Jacobs, Architect.

Right. Three windows wide and five stories high the brownstone occupies a slice of space on a busy New York City street. Entry to the building is at the lower right, a few steps below street level.

Below. The clean-lined fireplace wall is the focus for seating in the private rear living room. Sliding glass doors open to the sun court.

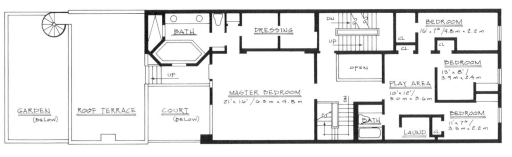

SECOND FLOOR

GARDEN (BELOW) | ROOF TERRACE | COURT (BELOW)

BATH | DRESSING | DN | UP | BEDROOM 16'·7"/4.8 m x 2.2 m

OPEN | BEDROOM 13'x 8'/ 3.9 m x 2.4 m

MASTER BEDROOM 21'x 16'/6.3 m x 4.8 m | PLAY AREA 10'x12'/ 3.0 m x 3.6 m

BATH | BEDROOM 11'x 7'/ 3.3 m x 2.2 m

LAUND. CL.

ENTRANCE LEVEL

GARDEN

LIVING ROOM 15'x 23'/4.5 m x 7.0 m | COURT

BREAKFAST 12'x 9'/ 3.8 m x 2.7 m | KITCHEN 16'x 9'/4.8 m x 2.7 m | DN | UP | ENTRY

CL.

DINING ROOM 21'x 16'/6.3 m x 4.8 m | GALLERY | LIBRARY 20'x 16'/6.1 m x 4.8 m

BATH

Above. The large dining room, open to view from the entry, doubles as a space for entertaining. Stairs, at left, lead to second floor bedrooms. The structural wall of brick was laid bare and painted white. A pivotal element on the main living level is the small sun court that opens on three sides to the dining, breakfast, and living rooms.

Photography note. The compactness of the interior space resulting from the long, narrow shape of the house again required the use of an extreme wide-angle lens to include meaningful amounts of each room in every composition. Since the sweep of the wide-angle lens is so great, special attention was paid to the placement of furniture so seating arrangements appear cohesive and not scattered about, unrelated to the architectural focus of the room. Special note was taken of elements near the edge of the picture to be sure they were recognizable.

Opposite page. The library at the front of the house also doubles as a guest room. Heavy, sliding paneled wood doors assure privacy. Track lighting illuminates the fireplace wall with its antique stone mantel.

Above left. In the upstairs master bedroom a bearing wall of revealed brick is a background for a marble fireplace saved in the renovation. The new inset wall across the back of the room includes a window that overlooks the court and a niche for a dressmaker's mannequin.

Above right. The dining table in the breakfast room off the kitchen is centered under a stained glass art-deco light fixture. The sunny court is in view here, too.

Lower left. Brightly patterned ceramic tiles decorate the floor and sunken, hexagonal tub of the master bath. A shower cubicle is at the right of the tub.

Cast in a Classical Mold

During the latter part of the nineteenth century the cast-iron facade building was a dominant architectural form in many cities of our country. The classical facades of arches and columns were run off in factories by the thousands as fronts for commercial and loft buildings. Despite a concerted effort to save these historic structures, many have been demolished. The one shown above was rescued on lower Broadway in New York City and the interior loft space remodeled into 144 duplex luxury and studio apartments. Stephen B. Jacobs, Architect.

Photography note. A main consideration in the photography of the interiors was to include the original, classical elements of the building in the overall room views—the fluted Corinthian columns and the high arched windows.

Above. In the remodeling process the exterior arcaded windows and prefabricated cast-iron front were left intact. Arcades of columns and arches are bearing walls for the corner building. The high, street-level floor (20′/6m) is devoted to shops and commercial use. The three high-ceilinged floors above contain double-height living rooms with sleeping balconies. At the top, two floors of living units were added where the original mansard roof stood.

Opposite page. The double-height living room borrows space from the sleeping loft above and the dining area and entry in the background. To the right is the kitchen. The classical columns are decorative monuments to an age when grace and tradition were a part of the building process.

Below. The Corinthian-style column shown here was considered the most ornate of the three Greek orders of architecture. The bell-shaped capital is enveloped with acanthus leaves. The sleeping loft overlooks the living room.

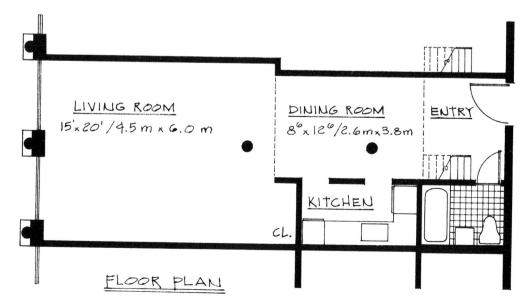

LIVING ROOM
15'×20'/4.5 m × 6.0 m

DINING ROOM
8⁶×12⁶/2.6m×3.8m

ENTRY

KITCHEN

CL.

FLOOR PLAN

Rebirth in Brooklyn

A Brooklyn brownstone built in the first decade of the twentieth century had seen many occupants and survived numerous interior alterations. When an architect and his family bought the house, they decided to occupy the top three floors themselves and maintain the basement level as a rental unit. A clearing-out process began that involved the removal of partitions and the blocking up of unnecessary doors and openings to give spaciousness and continuity to a previously jumbled interior. The first floor was allocated to the living room, dining room, and kitchen; the second floor was given over to bedrooms for two daughters; and the top level became the parents' domain. Nathan Smith, Architect.

Photography note. Extreme wide-angle lenses were necessary for photographing the narrow rooms (15'/4.4m wide). Some spaces were only about 6'/1.8m wide. The views of the open-planned living-dining area were carefully organized in order to show the space in meaningful proportions.

Left. The exterior of the four-story building remains virtually unchanged since its construction in 1908. The name brownstone, used synonymously with townhouse, derives from the reddish-brown sandstone used so frequently in masonry building.

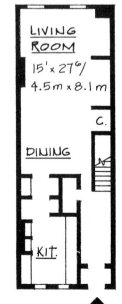

MAIN FLOOR

LIVING ROOM
15' x 27⁶/
4.5m x 8.1m

C.

DINING

KIT.

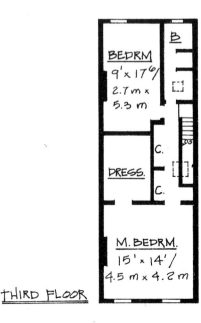

THIRD FLOOR

BEDRM
9' x 17⁶/
2.7m x 5.3m

B

C.

DRESS.

C.

M. BEDRM.
15' x 14'/
4.5m x 4.2m

Above. What had been a bedroom is now the new living room. The fireplace at left provides the focus for the furniture arrangement. Recessed ceiling lighting fixtures, a hanging fixture, and two tall windows at the end of the room brighten the space. A Moroccan rug is centered on a floor of teak parquet.

Below. A reverse view shows the dining area open to the living room and the entry hall to the left, and the kitchen to the right. Old wall coverings were removed to reveal the structural brick wall.

Opposite page. At the front of the house the kitchen occupies the space of the former sitting room and contains two banks of hinged shutters on the tall windows—open for light and shut for privacy. Butcher-block countertops with a lustrous wood grain complement the bright yellow steel cabinets below.

Above. The master bedroom on the third floor front is a rich mixture of bright colors—a yellow window wall and a red bedspread, deeply textured earthen hues of brick, and a collection of primitive art.

Left. The third-floor bedroom hall has one massive plane of brick that carries to the floor below. A skylight illuminates the stair shaft, and a wall of closets spans the length of the hallway at right.

4. Barns into Houses

The once proud days of the hard-working early American farm barn are near forgotten now. A Sunday drive in the country not too long ago would always bring at least a dozen of these brave mammoths into view. Today most are abandoned or in various stages of solitary neglect. Some, still in use, are relegated to the status of garages or storehouses and their existences suffered until they fall under their own weight.

Some satisfaction can be gained from the current interest in the remodeling of old barns into houses. While remodeling does not restore the original dignity and beauty of these buildings, it does at least preserve an impression of their vast spaces and leave much of their magnificent physical structure intact. People who take up the reclamation of these beautiful old structures are often drawn to them for their historicity, their tremendous interior spaces, and the wonderful old timbers that are exposed as part of the interior design. The four barns-now-houses included here have been treated respectfully by their owners and architects so that much of their former dignity has been salvaged.

New Jersey Tudor

A New Jersey barn (opposite) built in the early nineteenth century had almost expired when it was rescued by a home builder who could see its possibilities as a home for his family. Together he and a local architect who was well versed in the design and construction of early American buildings saved what was sound, replaced what had decayed, and added new materials to remodel the barn to a habitable dwelling that reflected its noble origins.

The before picture shows the exposed wood framing of the old barn, the raised foundation, and the haylofts on either side of the central two-story section that was reached by a ramp in the rear. The front of the barn was renovated in an English Tudor style, with handmade bricks and wood beams, sides faced with cedar boards, and a new roof of red cedar shingles. Stairs lead to an entry deck that spans the length of the house. William M. Thompson, Architect.

Photography note. Photographing 100-, 200-, and 300-year-old structures is a fascinating experience. One's eye is constantly caught by the beauty of the ancient wood and the fine craftsmanship of the joinery. The photographer has a double aim on these projects—to capture the living space as well as emphasize the structure.

An abundance of light is needed, at least 2,000 watts, to bring out the texture and grain of the wood that is the predominant material throughout. Since the wood surfaces are not polished, their often deeply textured gray tones absorb rather than reflect light. However, the barn framing of heavy posts and beams often contributes to arresting, strongly textured pictorial compositions. Again, in very small or high-ceilinged spaces, an extreme wide-angle lens is needed.

Opposite page. A view of the entry hall shows how the basic space arrangement of the barn was maintained. The center section of the house, an open shaft of space from the first floor to the roof, comprises the entry and family room. A balcony-bridge connects what were the haylofts of the original barn. Almost all the wood framing of the barn was retained and used in remodeling.

Below. The bay-windowed breakfast room has a splendid overhead of hand-hewn beams and rough-sawn joists. The old framing members have roman numerals chiseled into them to identify their position in the structure. In the background, small-paned, sliding glass doors open the family room to the rear deck.

Left. This bedroom, 10'6" x 14'/3.2m x 4.2m has space-saving bunks built with old timbers, and two storage drawers tuck under the lower bunk. Handmade bricks face the wall beyond the study niche.

Right. The master bedroom window matches the one in the breakfast room below. The window seat has a storage chest beneath it. The use of old framing members reinforces continuity of the barn theme in every room.

Opposite page. The dining room rendered in brick and timber echoes the entry elevation of the house. Wide-plank wood floors, wood-paneled wainscoting, and a colonial floral print wallpaper carry out the early American theme.

LIVING ROOM
21' x 21'/
6.3 m x 6.3 m

FAMILY ROOM
12' x 24'/
3.6 m x 7.3 m

BREAKFAST
18' x 9'/
5.4 m x 2.7 m

KITCHEN
18' x 11'/
5.4 m x 3.3 m

CARPORT
21' x 21'/
6.3 m x 6.3 m

UP

DN

REF. FR.

CL

CL

CL CL

STUDY
11' x 14'
3.3 m x 4.2 m

UP

ENTRY

DINING ROOM
18' x 15'/
5.4 m x 4.5 m

DN

FIRST FLOOR PLAN

DECK

BEDROOM - 2
11' x 18' /
3.3 m x 5.4 m

BEDROOM - 3
10' x 14' /
3.2 m x 4.2 m

OPEN

MASTER
BEDROOM
18' x 13' /
5.4 m x 3.9 m

CL

CL

CL

CL

UP   DN

UP

DRESSING

ROOF BELOW

BRIDGE

BATH

BEDROOM - 4
11' x 13' /
3.3 m x 3.9 m

BATH

OPEN

SEWING AREA
18' x 7' /
5.4 m x 5.2 m

SECOND FLOOR PLAN

Above. In the family room at the back of the full-height center section of the house, barn doors stood where the wall of glass is now. Haywagons reached the raised first level of the barn via a ramp beyond the barn doors. The massive brick chimney carries the eye upward to the peak of the barn roof.

Opposite page. A detail of the front exterior of the house shows the Tudor treatment of brick and timber. An "eyebrow" canopy protects the front door.

Up to Date in a Seventeenth-Century Cow Barn

What was originally a cow barn located near the east end of Long Island, New York is now a year-round home for a family whose ancestors have occupied the land for ten generations—since about 1640. For a number of years the present generation and their children lived in the main house facing the main street of the village. Plans were formulated to convert the 300-year-old cow barn into a studio for the husband, but his childhood memories of the old building were so pleasant that the decision was made to sell the big house on the street and remodel the barn for the family's new home. Edward W. Slater, Architect.

Below. Additions were made to the basic two-story structure of the barn. The dining room with a shed roof, at the right of the living room, was originally a chicken coop. Behind the dining room is an extension containing the kitchen and playroom. At the opposite end of the house two bedrooms were added.

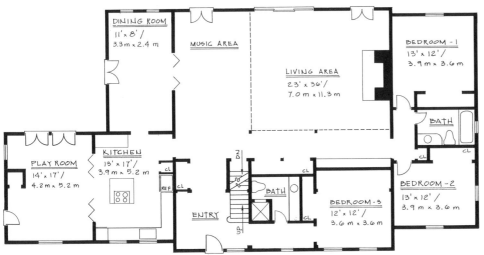

FIRST FLOOR PLAN

Opposite page. Floor-to-ceiling glass in living room occupies the space of the original barn doors seen in the exterior view of the back of the new house. These centered, roof-high, double doors are typical of almost all barns built on the eastern end of Long Island. To the right of the window are some of the original hand-hewn posts and beams retained in the remodeling.

Opposite page. Full height of the barn structure was retained in the renovation of the interior. Hand-adzed posts and beams support the balcony master bedroom suite that overlooks the living room on two sides. Sliding barn doors close to separate the bedroom from the living area.

Left. A new skylight illuminates the entry foyer. Original timbers retain the barn flavor as frames around doorways and skylight and as the wall plate that supports the roof rafters. Flagstones with cement joints make up the floor.

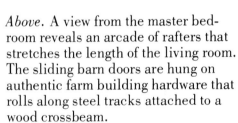

Above. A view from the master bedroom reveals an arcade of rafters that stretches the length of the living room. The sliding barn doors are hung on authentic farm building hardware that rolls along steel tracks attached to a wood crossbeam.

Left. Stairs lead from foyer to the second floor that comprises the parents' domain with private bath, dressing area, bedroom, and a small reading nook—the railinged area over the hall to the living room.

Stable to Home

When the owner-designer started remodeling this nineteenth-century Connecticut barn-stable, his main task was to clean out a hundred-year-old accumulation of debris. An inspection of the framing and foundation revealed the parts that could be retained and those that would have to be discarded and replaced. From the beginning the project was one of exploration and discovery, guided by the desire to retain the essence of the original structure and use the exposed interior as part of the finished project. Michael Greenberg, Designer-builder.

Above. The exterior of the old barn was restored with board siding found on many old barns through New England. Much of the exterior framing had to be replaced, but the supporting stone pillars were in good condition. A temporary scaffolding held up the structure while new posts and beams took the place of the rotted ones. All the posts, beams, and framing members used in the remodeling were a part of the original building or gathered from demolished barns in New England.

Right. The living room fireplace was newly built from native stone.

Opposite page. The open-planned interior of the main body of the barn is comprised of the living room, kitchen, and the second-story sleeping loft. The tongue-and-groove pine boards that cover the walls were retained from the old stable. New sliding glass doors open to a small sitting deck. A private bedroom-study is reached through the kitchen.

Opposite page. The open sleeping loft was built anew from framing gathered from other old barns. A feeling of great spaciousness in the interior belies the fact that the main structure is only 31' x 24'/9.8m x 7.4m. The shape of the gambrel roof is articulated inside by the roof framing that stands out in bold relief against white ceiling planes. The builder-owner uses a part of the sleeping balcony as office space.

Above left. The barn motif is not interrupted even in the kitchen, with its abundance of aged wood surfaces. Under-counter cabinet doors are made from barn siding and hinged with wrought-iron straps. A center-island table has a butcher-block top.

Above right. Surely the rain barrel tub-shower in the main-level bathroom is one of a kind—lined with waterproof fiberglass and its door hinged with straps of leather.

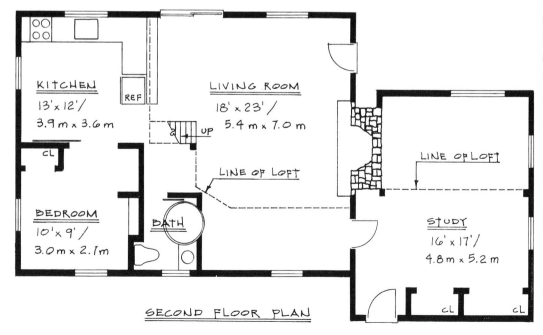

KITCHEN
13' x 12'/
3.9 m x 3.6 m

CL

BEDROOM
10' x 9'/
3.0 m x 2.1 m

LIVING ROOM
18' x 23'/
5.4 m x 7.0 m

UP

LINE OF LOFT

BATH

LINE OF LOFT

STUDY
16' x 17'/
4.8 m x 5.2 m

CL   CL

SECOND FLOOR PLAN

Hessian Hostelry

Built over 200 years ago near Long Island Sound, north of New York City, this beautiful old barn was initially designed for threshing grain. The original roof-high doors at the front and back could be opened to the prevailing southwest winds that would blow away the chaff as the farmers flailed the stalks of grain. These doors have now been partially filled in.

The old barn has also shared in some of the more dramatic action of American history. During the Revolutionary War, Hessian soldiers on their way to the Battle of White Plains landed their

boats a few hundred yards away and may have entered the barn while reconnoitering. Also, the local town militia was quartered in the barn during the War of 1812 when the British fleet stood offshore in the Sound. Leonard Weinberg, Architect.

Above. The hand-planed cedar shingles on the front of the house are a part of the original construction. Each shingle is 3 ft/1m long, with just 8 in/200mm exposed to the weather. As is the case with most remodeled barns, the basic structure was supplemented with parts from many other colonial buildings. Two eighteenth-century taverns, for instance, supplied the bricks for the fireplace and the oak flooring used for kitchen cabinets. From a house built in a nearby town came the Palladian window over the front door.

Opposite page. A strong sense of the original structure is seen in the kitchen with its ceiling of 2″/50mm-thick floor boards and hand-adzed beams. Two-hundred-year-old oak flooring planks are used to face the cabinets. The countertop is one continuous slab of wood 2′/.6m wide, with cambium layer and bark still intact. Flooring is of clay tile.

Below. The dining room is furnished with a varied selection of early American pieces. An antique piano in the shape of a clavichord stands against the back wall.

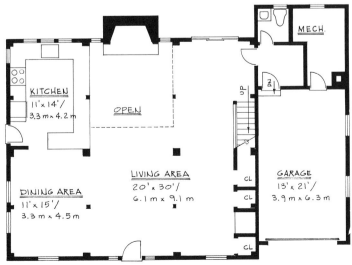

FIRST FLOOR PLAN

SECOND FLOOR PLAN

Opposite. The master bedroom area spans the full depth of the house over the dining room and kitchen. A view from the storage nook over the dressing room shows the great volume of space in the roof-high room. The lower flight of stairs leads from the balcony-level landing to the bedroom proper. Sound and heat insulation between roof rafters is made of dark brown slabs of cork-particle board to match the wood framing.

Below. The bedroom hall at the top of the stairs from the first level shows typical barn framing. All the basic construction consists of native white and red oak planks with pegged joints. The major dimensions in the structure are in multiples of three—or "Trinity" proportions, as they were called.

5. Outbuildings

Existing secondary structures such as garages, stables, and utility buildings present an excellent opportunity for the expansion of living space. Their separateness is an advantage when privacy or seclusion is called for. Also there is sometimes no practical way to add on to the house proper.

If the outbuilding is in reasonable repair, the most important elements of its construction are already in place: footings, foundation, floors, walls, and roof. Even one or more utilities—electricity, water, sewage—may have been previously installed.

The three annex buildings shown in this chapter are examples of how an attic over a stable was turned into an income-producing apartment; a garage was remodeled into a guest-pool house; and a new outbuilding was erected to house a family activities center.

Stable Attic into Spacious Apartment

The space under the roof of this outbuilding (opposite) had gone virtually unused for many years until the owner recognized its potential as an income-producing or guest apartment.

The interior of the second floor was in the typical unfinished state of any old attic. Roof rafters, collar beams, and wall studs were all exposed. The main construction work involved the application of finished surfaces: plasterboard ceilings, plywood walls, and wall-to-wall carpeting throughout. The installation of the necessary wiring and piping was accomplished before the finishing was begun.

The stable faces a large graveled parking area. The two openings at right are now used for cars; entry door to the upstairs apartment is in the center, and the two horse stalls are at the left end. Two dormers in the roof were already in place. Louise P. Rosenfeld, Designer, ASID; Roger S. Blaho, Architect.

Photography note. The photography of the building presented no special problems with the exception of the entry stairway. The floor area at the bottom of the stairs is about 4′ x 5′/1.2m x 1.6m—barely enough room to set up a tripod. To get the full rise of the steps, the camera had to be about 3′/1m above floor level and an extreme wide-angle lens used to get the full height of the close-up subject. Care was taken to include the free-standing fireplace in both views of the living-dining area so the connection between the spaces could be seen.

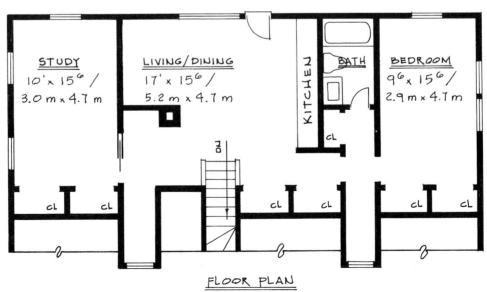

STUDY
10' x 15⁶ /
3.0 m x 4.7 m

LIVING/DINING
17' x 15⁶ /
5.2 m x 4.7 m

KITCHEN

BATH

BEDROOM
9⁶ x 15⁶ /
2.9 m x 4.7 m

CL

DN

CL CL CL CL CL CL

FLOOR PLAN

Opposite page. The stable is set into a hill so the second story is at ground level in the rear. One of the few structural changes made in the remodeling was the installation of the floor-to-ceiling colonial window that lights the living-dining area.

Above. Roof-high ceiling in the living-dining area gives an amazing spaciousness to this central section of the apartment. A prefabricated metal fireplace and flue are hooked into the existing masonry chimney.

Below. A one-piece kitchen unit fits in the slender space behind folding doors. The unit is composed of a range, oven, refrigerator, sink, and storage. Closets line one wall of the house under the eaves where the head room is too low for normal use of floor space. Plumbing for the bath and kitchen is ganged in one wall to save materials and labor costs.

Garage to Guest House

A Long Island, New York family who had recently built a swimming pool on their property found they soon needed facilities to accommodate afternoon and overnight guests. They discovered that their nearby garage, a handsome structure of brick and shingle, was much more suitable for housing people than engines. Nancy Brous, Designer; Arthur Klonsky & Associates, Landscape designers.

Right. A wide roof dormer expanded space upstairs to make room for two bedrooms, a bath, and sauna. A brick planter wall and a flagstone-topped barbecue flank the new terrace, with the sliding glass doors making the terrace and the living room one continuous space.

Below. In the open-planned living-dining room, white is the background for a red nylon carpet and red and blue striped shades and cushions of shiny vinyl—all resistant to moisture.

Right. During remodeling, the garage still had its one-car opening that was made into a dining room window. The new dormer is at the sheathing stage of construction. Work on the terrace has not yet begun.

Below. Director's chairs with seats and backs of vinyl seat a party of eight in the dining area. A softly curved valance follows the arch of the original lintel, and a novel stair treatment can be seen in the use of cast-iron piping sections for the newel post and the railings. The glassed-in garage door opening gives a view of the property.

Photography note. Photographing the two interior stories of this guest house remodeling presented subjects of space that were direct opposites. The ground floor living level was one open area; the second floor was made up of two small bedrooms. Downstairs, two opposite corners of the open-planned living-dining area were chosen as the best camera positions to show how the space was apportioned for separate uses. To illustrate the relationship between the two areas, two dining chairs were included in the view of the living area. Upstairs, the camera was placed as tightly into a corner as possible, and an extreme wide-angle lens used. A low camera position minimized the smallness of the rooms.

Above. An upstairs bedroom for a lady guest is decorated with a floral background of bright reds and yellows and window and sofa fabric of blue patent vinyl. The cushioned headboard for the sofa-bed is suspended from a wooden curtain rod. A full-height ceiling is made possible by the new dormer extension.

Right. For the male guest the second upstairs bedroom has walls clad in dark brown plywood with baseboard heating units painted to match. The fabric for the shades and sofa-bed is black-and-white check.

Barn Building Family Room

Sometimes the construction of a new outbuilding is called for when it is not feasible to add to the primary house and there is no other dependent structure on the property. Such was the case with this two-hundred-year-old New England colonial home. F. Lincoln Geiffert, Architect.

The exterior of the new family room structure is fashioned in a barn motif and also adheres to the colonial detailing of the main house. The nearness of the main road to the front of the house, less than 20′/6m away, and the rocky site made an addition to the original structure impractical. A fan light over the front door sheds light on the raised loft area within.

Opposite page. The interior of the new family room is immense in volume and contrasts dramatically and intentionally with the small, confined rooms of the main house. Focus for the furniture arrangement in the sitting area is the used brick fireplace. Light floods the room through the high small-paned window.

Above. A corner kitchen equipped for light entertaining is tucked under the loft area which is reached by ladder. The exposed roof framing defines the high ceiling. Barn siding and beams taken from an old farmhouse across the road authenticate the colonial theme of the design.

Below. Barn siding is used in the kitchen on the cupboard and closet doors and wall surfaces. A steel sink with raised spout is recessed in the plastic laminate counter; below, a small refrigerator has a decorative front panel of simulated barn siding.

Photography note. Photographing large, one-room spaces requires exact planning of each view before any photography is actually done. All important aspects of the space must be shown, but without repetitive overlapping that would tend to make one picture look much like another. However, minimum duplication is necessary to show how adjoining areas relate to each other. The most difficult camera position to select was the one depicting the new and old exteriors. The proximity of the structures to a main roadway demanded a position far enough away to include at least half the original building and all of the new. A comprehensive exterior view was hampered by numerous trees and utility poles that lined the street in front of the house.

6. Adding On...and On

Sometimes homeowners never leave well enough alone—to their great satisfaction. They start with a good idea and keep improving on it. This type of long-term nurturing of a home is quite different from a one-time remodeling project. The key to adding on is to start with a basic house on a great site in a good neighborhood or community and then develop the structure to suit the needs of the occupants and the value of the land. In doing this, the limits of the existing structure must always be considered and the new structure must be a workable extension of the old. The two houses shown here had humble beginnings, but given considerable care over the years they have developed into homes of substance and individuality.

From Cottage to Luxury Home

Transformation of this originally simple dwelling in Putnam County, New York (opposite) into an extensively enlarged luxury home took place in two major stages. The floor plan was left virtually intact during the first stage, but was rearranged during the second. Careful attention was given throughout to the use of natural materials and a strong horizontal emphasis to unite the house with the site.

The first step was to remodel the exterior. The old clapboard box was given a new facing of stucco, stone pillars, and horizontal wood trim; the asphalt roof was clad with red cedar shingles and extended with a gabled trellis; and a new cantilevered deck extended the living space outdoors. All the grounds around the house were heavily planted with evergreens and ivy and graded and terraced with planters, retaining walls, and steps built of railroad ties. Frank Edward Dushin, Architect.

Photography note. This two-stage remodeling was photographed on two occasions several years apart. The object of the first photographic session was to show the exterior changes that had been made to the basic cabin. Since no interior remodeling had been done at this time, the exterior photography was considerable, especially in view of the planting and landscape construction done. The photography of the second stage had to clearly delineate the relationship of the new, long wing to the original structure as well as show the new and remodeled interior spaces. The complexity of this type of project demanded a well-thought-out shooting script before the actual photography began.

Below. Extended exposed rafters with a shadeboard edge cast delicate shadow and light patterns on the laths of vertical redwood that march down the glassed bedroom hallway. The garden is composed of a deep mulch of cedar chips overlaid with rocks, and evergreen plantings of andromeda, rhododendron. and juniper.

Opposite page. A flagstone entry was added in the first stage of the remodeling. This end of the house matches the "before" picture and is at the opposite side of the house from the deck addition. The deep roof overhang adds apparent length to the house and gathers the terrace sitting area into the structure. Extensive development of the grounds with railroad ties, stone walls, and planting makes the outdoors an architectural part of the structure.

Below. The second stage of the remodeling, (see plans below) involved a long, right-angle extension to the house and the rearrangement of the floor plan in the original structure. Stone, stucco, and low, sloping roof planes continue the design theme of the first-stage change. The use of natural materials and a strong horizontal emphasis unite the house with the site.

Opposite page. The addition of the deck made an outdoor living room that was part of the floor plan, with built-in seating incorporated as part of the deck railing. Both the deck and the roof extension give the house a strong three-dimensional quality that was lacking before the remodeling. Two sets of sliding glass doors, at right in photo, open to the master bedroom and the living room.

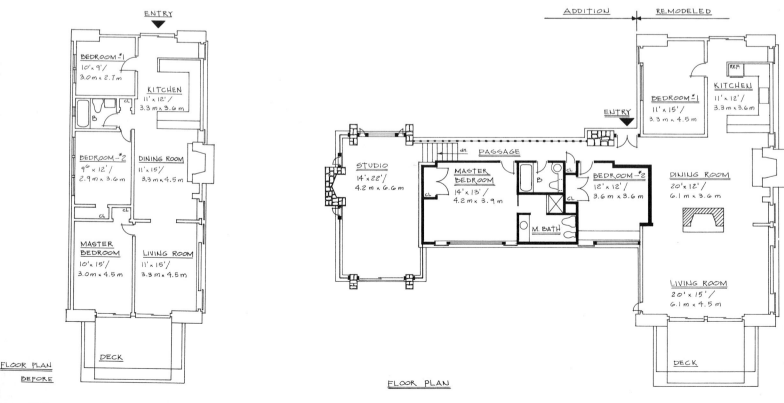

FLOOR PLAN
BEFORE

FLOOR PLAN

Above. A view from the front of the house shows the studio end of the second stage. The long, low extension fits snugly to the site and ties the entire building intimately to the grounds. A strong sense of shelter and privacy is provided by the broad, low-sloping roof and the deep overhangs. The organic flavor and fine detailing of the wood and stone work are reminiscent of much of the work of Frank Lloyd Wright. The transition between house and grounds is executed with particular subtlety.

Right. The studio is lower than the rest of the main living level making it a tall, light-filled space. Stone, wood, and glass are highlighted against a background of plain white, with the stone masses of the pillars and the chimney working as part of both the interior and exterior design.

Opposite page top. Space that once included the living room and master bedroom was remodeled in the second stage to comprise one large living room. The large ceiling beam spanning the length of the room shows where the partition was located. Both sets of sliding glass doors extend the living room onto the outside deck. Modern furnishings befit the new contemporary interiors.

Above. A massive stone fireplace is the interior focus for the arrangement of the living room furniture. Space flows between living and dining rooms on either side of the central stone divider.

Left. The new dining room also spans the full width of the primary structure. Broad planes of white give a face-lift to the old fireplace in the background, and the wall of native stone that decorates the dining room is the rear face of the living room fireplace chimney.

Adding Ad Infinitum

A concert pianist and his family bought a small suburban house on a private wooded site in Westchester County, New York, and enlarged it to accommodate his domestic and professional needs. What was once a post-World War II basic shelter is now a spacious contemporary of great variety and interest. F. Lincoln Geiffert, Architect.

Below. Two low-sloping gables instead of one face front in the updated version of the house. The original body of the house is at the right, the piano studio addition is at left, with a flat-roofed entry between the two winged masses.

Right. The studio is airy and bright with exposed-beam ceiling and walls of glass front and back. This professional space is separate from the rest of the house so that students can come and go without disturbing the family.

Opposite page above. Originally, the living room extended only as far as the vertical post that supports the roof's ridge beam. Enclosing the porch was a relatively inexpensive procedure, since the floor, foundation, framing, and roof were already in place.

Opposite page below. The "before" view shows the front elevation before the living room was extended to include the open porch. Second stage addition: an entrance foyer, half bath, dining room, and a piano instruction studio. Third stage addition: an enclosed solarium replaced a screened porch and a breakfast room was included in the kitchen space.

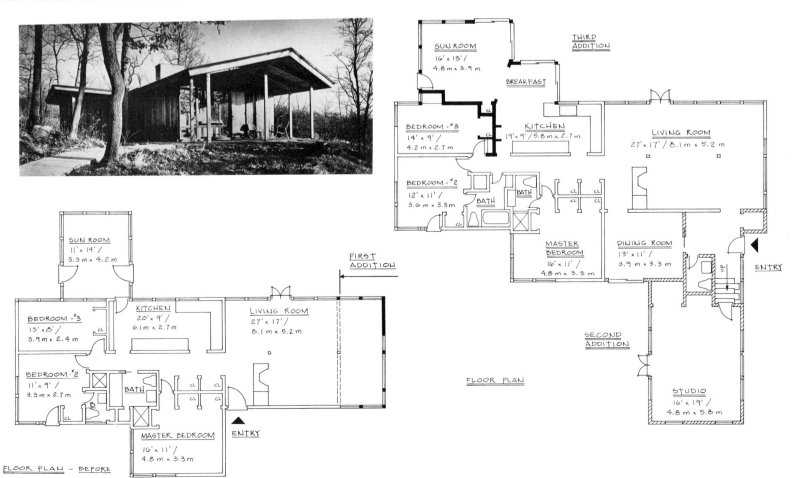

SUN ROOM
16' x 13' /
4.8 m x 3.9 m

THIRD
ADDITION

BREAKFAST

BEDROOM - #3
14' x 9' /
4.2 m x 2.7 m

KITCHEN
19' x 9' / 5.8 m x 2.7 m

LIVING ROOM
27' x 17' / 8.1 m x 5.2 m

BEDROOM - #2
12' x 11' /
3.6 m x 3.3 m

BATH

BATH

MASTER
BEDROOM
16' x 11' /
4.8 m x 3.3 m

DINING ROOM
13' x 11' /
3.9 m x 3.3 m

ENTRY

FLOOR PLAN

SECOND
ADDITION

STUDIO
16' x 19' /
4.8 m x 5.8 m

SUN ROOM
11' x 14' /
3.3 m x 4.2 m

FIRST
ADDITION

BEDROOM - #3
13' x 8' /
3.9 m x 2.4 m

KITCHEN
20' x 9' /
6.1 m x 2.7 m

LIVING ROOM
27' x 17' /
8.1 m x 5.2 m

BEDROOM - #2
11' x 9' /
3.3 m x 2.7 m

BATH

MASTER BEDROOM
16' x 11' /
4.8 m x 3.3 m

ENTRY

FLOOR PLAN - BEFORE

125

Above. The south-facing side of the
house has windows along its entire
length for light and warmth. This side
of the house also overlooks the new
swimming pool. From left to right are
the living room, kitchen, breakfast
room, and sun room.

Right. When the new sun room was
added in the third stage, the adjoining
child's bedroom lost a couple of windows, but gained privacy and a built-in
study-desk niche. The roof-high ceilings in the small bedroom give a
needed feeling of spaciousness.

Left. The revamped kitchen seems much larger than it did in the original house because it is now part of the continuous space that includes the breakfast room and the sun room. The exposed rafters and beams give the interiors architectural interest.

Below. As in most homes the kitchen and adjacent spaces seem the most attractive for the day's informal activities. The breakfast room is the center for over-coffee conversation and has pleasant views both inside and out.

Photography note. Photographing this multiple-stage remodeling required close consultation with the architect and a careful examination of the working drawings to find what parts of the structure were unchanged, what areas of the original structure had been altered, and what was entirely new.

The main photographic emphasis was on the areas of change. Since the remodeling was executed in the same style and with similar materials as the basic house, a good written description and accompanying floor plans were a necessary complement to the photographs. The aim of the photographic coverage was to show the design changes clearly without resorting to an unmanageable quantity of pictures.

7. Little Out of Pocket

Saving money will always be in style, and good ideas are always most welcome as shown by the rooms assembled in this chapter. While the penny-wise approach may not be suitable for all situations, thrift coupled with imagination has proved most appropriate for informal living spaces, children's and guest rooms, and vacation houses. Inventiveness, a sense of humor, an eye for a bargain, and a little legerdemain are all that is required to make a lot from a little.

Flair on a Budget

The rooms shown opposite and on the next two pages are guest rooms in an inn on eastern Long Island, New York. The owner of the inn designed the rooms himself. His primary intention was to find a good, easily executed idea. He accomplished this by using decorative materials to achieve a three-dimensional architectural effect.

He implemented his schemes with a generous and bold use of color, the refinishing of "found" furnishings, and the architectural effects of trompe l'oeil. Brilliant mustard yellow is the motif in the bed-sitting room—used on walls, ceiling, and wicker chairs. A three-dimensional effect of a classical denticulated cornice is achieved with wallpaper at the ceiling edge, window valances, and the coffee table. The old wicker chairs and table were restored with sandpaper and paint. Farrell Gilmore, Designer-owner.

Photography note. The focus for the camera in shooting the subject matter for this chapter was slightly different from the usual rendering of architectural space. The theme of thrift was central to each composition rather than the capturing of volume, shape, and detail. Camera position, lighting, choice of lens, and the arrangement of furniture and accessories were all coordinated to emphasize ingenuity of design accomplished with limited funds.

Above. Sawed-off wood ladders are used as headboards for two sofa-beds. "Structural" posts and beams are 1″ x 6″/25mm x 150mm pine boards painted olive green and nailed to the gypsum wall board.

Right. The headboard wall of this bedroom is the decorative focus for an otherwise unadorned space. Pine boards colored a brilliant blue against a wall of white invoke a regimental theme. The necessary red, in a glossy enamel, is applied to a reclaimed Victorian dresser.

Opposite page. Another view of the yellow bed-sitting room shows how a kitchenette is partitioned off with old window shutters hinged together and painted. The trompe l'oeil cornice molding is continued around the four walls. All the paintings are by Bart Clancy.

Much Overhead

Opposite page. The daughter of an interior designer wanted to redecorate her bedroom a little differently. She succeeded, in collaboration with her mother, in building a giant ceiling collage made up of memorabilia and bits and pieces of things. Some of the elements of the three-dimensional design are: radio parts, electrical wiring equipment, plywood shapes, sheet music, posters, rug samples, cattails, packing cartons, toys, champagne bottles, and trophies.

Above. Along the wood paneled wall of the bedroom a work center includes bookshelves, a long counter for hobbies and homework, and plenty of drawer space. At the far end of the 10′ x 16′/3m x 5m room are two clothes closets. Louise P. Rosenfeld, Designer, ASID.

Eureka! The Attic

Making dead attic space work as a full partner in the floor plan is like finding money in the street. Working boldly with a few materials the designer turned a room full of roof rafters into a bedroom for her son at minimum expense. The new circular steel staircase saves space in both the attic and the floor below. Louise P. Rosenfeld, Designer, ASID.

Right. The bed fits neatly under the low headroom of the slanting roof plane, with barn siding adding a touch of rusticity and masculinity. At the end of the bed an old oak desk acts as a divider between the living and sleeping areas.

Below. The 14′ x 24′/4.2m x 7.4m attic provided ample space for a large sitting area. Bold patterned fabrics and posters cover the entire side walls. Old French doors make a generous end-wall window.

Left. A wide, roll-down window shade is built in over the French doors and has a double duty: on hot summer days it blocks the sun's heat and it also works as a projection screen for slides and movies. The indoor-outdoor carpeting can take much abuse.

8. Industry at Home

Building materials and equipment used in industrial construction are rarely seen in residential building. The two realms have always been considered antithetical and incompatible. The word industrial readily connotes images of harshness, raw efficiency, utilitarianism, and wearisome labor—all alien to the visions of comfort, cheer, and warmth associated with home.

But, there are other aspects of industrial materials that make them quite appropriate for home building, particualry in contemporary homes. Many components of factory buildings have a spare and functional character, a simplicity and forthrightness that give them an honest and unobtrusive elegance. And because they are designed to do a job in a highly critical and demanding production environment, it is likely they will perform efficiently and reliably with a minimum of maintenance. Industrial building materials probably cost less because of their lack of adornment and lower marketing overhead costs. George van Geldern, Architect for all houses in this chapter.

Small Panes on a Grand Scale

A living room (opposite) with a grand panorama of wooded hills and valleys to the west has two stories of steel factory windows to capture the view and light. Woven translucent shades roll down to cut the sky glare in the afternoon when the sun is strong. The windows have inset panels that swing open for fresh air. Thin muntins of steel interrupt the view only slightly, but have the great advantage of making glass replacement inexpensive if the window is broken.

Photography note. The photographs in this section are essentially dual-purpose. Each view was carefully composed to show an important interior space and, at the same time, highlight the function and appearance of an industrial building material used there.

Sheet Metal Decoration

Above. Exposed metal flues ventilate the living room fireplace and, to the right, the furnace in the basement. The prefabricated metal fireplace has a cement plaster finish applied at the site. The flues can be treated similarly. The great advantage of exposing the flues is that they radiate otherwise lost heat to the house interior.

Breakfast Bauhaus Style

Below. Factory windows are used on a small scale in an intimate, "tree house" breakfast room. The windows can be ordered in almost any increment of the basic pane dimensions. The simplicity of the window design fits most comfortably with the architect's highly imaginative, yet informal approach to architecture—the ceiling and corner trim of unfinished, rough-sawn cedar boards and the flooring of natural clay tiles.

Conduits in the Kitchen

Opposite page. Overhead, rectangular framework of pipe conduits channel electrical wiring to tiny floodlights that illuminate a contemporary kitchen. This kind of lightbulb is often used for commercial displays. The ceiling-hung pipe racks obviously have an important second virtue in their capacity to store large containers within easy reach. The bare-boned functionalism of the design has a tacit decorative quality of playfulness about it.

Billboard Lighting

Above. Another new idea in kitchen illuminations is use of large reflector lights that were originally designed for manufacturing and billboard installations. The angled, white porcelain-enamel reflectors direct glare away from the kitchen worker's eyes and light the walls and countertop work areas.

Flights of Steel

Opposite page. A factory staircase painted a bright blue crisscrosses a central shaft of space and connects four levels in a contemporary interior. The open-tread and railing design gives the eye an omnidirectional view from the entry level to the rooftop, making modest space seemingly immense. The unprepossessing quality of the staircase is in harmony with the simply detailed wood framing, trim, walls, and ceilings.

9. Home Offices

Not too many years ago the home office in the average house consisted of a desk at one end of the living room. With the increasing complexity of life (papers and forms to fill out for almost everything) the need for a private, organized working area at home has become essential for a great many people.

The best offices seem to be those that are planned when the rest of the house is being designed. At this time adequate space for work and storage can be reserved in an area away from the noise and traffic of daily living. Provision can be made for files, a safe, telephone equipment, and special electrical equipment such as an adding machine, tape recorder, copier, and typewriter.

The size and detailing of the home office will depend on the amount and kind of work done there—from managing domestic affairs to conducting a full-time business.

Nest-High Desk

Designed as part of a house addition, this balcony office (opposite) overlooks the master bedroom that, itself, is in a secluded part of the house. The private stairway at left is the only access to the work area. The view through the openable skylight shows the aerie quality of the space. Note the three different counter heights for various tasks. Robert H. King, Architect.

Photography note. The photography of the home office usually has to be accomplished in one picture, since it is just one room of many that has to fit in an article layout. Thus a viewpoint should be chosen that will show the most important elements of the working area and also be a comprehensive composition of the architectural space. A wide-angle lens should be considered as the most adaptable for this situation. A good amount of tidying up will probably be necessary to give the office a workmanlike but serene appearance. Even a moderate amount of clutter in a room will result in a very messy looking photograph. The eye tends to edit out a confusion of objects, whereas the camera lens will not.

Library-Office

Above. Ready reference was the basic design consideration in the planning of this home office where both husband and wife research and write professionally. Bookcases cover three walls of the room, and the vertical dividers have notched tracks on their sides that permit the shelf heights to be adjusted. Space-saving staircase leads to the third-floor room. The openness of the design interferes minimally with the library. The wide-plank pine floor is part of the 150-year-old structure. Louise P. Rosenfeld, Designer, ASID.

Balcony Retreat

Opposite page. A balcony overlooking the master bedroom is again chosen by an architect as an ideal location for an office. The vertical window blinds repeat the narrow-board ceiling motif. The background pattern of light and shadow changes as the sun crosses the sky, and the quiet and seclusion of the room is almost palpable. Paul J. Mitarachi, Architect.

Integral Design Scheme

Opposite page. A bright and airy home office for an interior designer was custom designed for her as part of an addition to her house. The advantages of planning a home work space as part of a total structural scheme are apparent here. All the design requirements for the room are considered concurrently, making a finished product of perfectly interrelated parts. Anne Wright Wilson, Designer.

Two-Gabled Office

Above. The steeply sloping roofs of older houses shelter roomy attic spaces, and what the attic may lack in convenience, it more than makes up for in an abundance of ready-to-remodel space. Two intersecting, right-angle gables dictated the L-shaped floor plan of this tree-top-level office. By glazing each gable end, the owner brought light, view, and spaciousness to the interior. Arthur Watkins, Designer.

High-Rise Elegance

Below. The home office of an advertising executive has a touch of Madison Avenue formality with space allotted to both seating-conference and deskwork areas. A selection of photographics decorates the wall above the sofa. Wood ladders frame the bookshelves and make top shelves accessible. George van Geldern, Architect.

10. Artists at Home

Home studios of professional artists are a delight to visit because they are such highly personal and specialized places. Unlike the living spaces in most houses, which are designed as habitation for many, the studio is usually planned for the exclusive use of one person and is most functional when designed around the working routine of the artist. The studio is not a passive room—not a place just to be occupied. It is both a retreat and a command headquarters where the artist, in isolation, must struggle to cajole and please his own particular muse. Even when the working room is in repose, one can imagine the hours of preparation, moments of inspiration, and the feverish activity of creation.

The six home studios in this section belong to pictorial artists who work in painting, illustration, architecture, and theatrical stage design. In all but one case the studios are remodelings of or additions to existing space.

Second-Story Studio

A many-times-remodeled colonial barn building is now a studio for two. Husband/architect and painter/wife work, both separately and simultaneously, in its newly revitalized interior. For several years the architect used the space in its original state as an office but removal of the ceiling inspired a host of changes so attractive that his wife also moved in with easel, canvases, and paints.

All the space framed by the structure (opposite) is now a part of the studio. Above the old ceiling the original, handcut roof beams are accented by white panels of plasterboard. Triangular spaces on two sides of the chimney are storage areas for frames and canvases. The trim and cabinets were painted white to avoid detracting from the rich textures of the barn siding that was retained as the wall covering.

Beyond the door are a guest room and bath that can be reached by a separate entrance. The architect's drafting table is at the right. F. Lincoln Geiffert, Architect.

Photography note. The photography of the structures and spaces in this chapter was done primarily from an architectural point of view rather than one of human interest. Thus all the work-a-day clutter was neatly arranged or stored away before photographing began. Everything was made neat for publication—often to the consternation of the occupant.

Above. In the sitting area a sofa-bed rests on two sets of three-drawer plan files. An eclectic window arrangement includes an antique fanlight and a contemporary skylight. Interior space that was once oppressive is now free.

Below. Before remodeling, the architect used the second-story of the barn pretty much as he found it. The low, boldly figured ceiling could hardly be ignored. Opening the room to the full height of the roof doubled the apparent space. Aged and deeply etched, the original barn siding was retained on the walls.

Clerestory Work Room

Opposite page. A studio for a painter was part of the architect's plans for a contemporary house. Disliking complete isolation while she worked, the painter had the studio located above and behind the living room with an opening between. A private stairway rises from the main living level of the house. The two-story-high room has abundant light and storage for finished canvases occupies one corner of the studio from floor to ceiling. A simple framework of notched vertical pine boards makes plywood shelves adjustable to fit various sizes of paintings. Robert H. King, Architect.

Back Porch Atelier

A magazine and advertising illustrator who preferred working at home to commuting to the city remodeled a jalousie-windowed back porch into a most efficient and comfortable work space. The new studio projects at a right angle from the rear of the house and can be closed to interruption during working hours. To insure quiet and isolation the architect conceived the addition as an annex to the main body of the house rather than an integral part of the plan, yet the studio opens freely to the wooded private back yard. Spencer M. Johnson, Architect.

Right. A simple contemporary form, the new studio is painted in a subdued dark brown to fit easily and unobtrusively with its Tudor parent structure. The three-paned clerestory window scoops in north light.

Above. Bookshelves line the wall of the studio facing the terrace. Over the shelves lights can be placed where desired on a continuous electrified track. The ceiling and walls are covered with random-width pine boards painted white—the same material used for the exterior siding. A high-gloss finish to the wood parquet floor tiles gives the room a certain elegance.

Below. The designer's center of operations is well equipped for serious work. Storage cabinets with a shelf above line the wall. Two large tables hold paints, brushes, canvases, and paper. A high-intensity fluorescent lighting fixture hangs from the ceiling to illuminate the working area. Examples of the artist's work hang on the barn-sided rear wall.

Paints in the Attic

The top floor of a 100-year-old Victorian house has been remodeled into a light-filled contemporary classroom, studio, and second living area. The rest of the house was restored to its 1870s ambiance, complete with period furnishings and accessories. F. Lincoln Geiffert, Architect.

Above. Houses of Victorian vintage have found great favor with remodelers, not only for their antique flavor, but also for the great volumes of space, high ceilings, and tall windows.

Above right. White and skylights relieve the gloom of the ancient attic. Two crossbeams replace many small collar beams to support the weight of the roof on the outer walls. A large leather sofa divides the sitting and work areas. The original brick chimney was left untouched.

Below right. Paintings, free-standing fireplace and the television are a focus for the seating arrangement in the accessible living room. A six-sided bay window holds an old wooden calliope horse.

Opposite page. A large skylight illuminates the studio work center which is in the northwest corner of the attic. Easel, tools, and desk are all within easy reach for the busy mother, artist, teacher.

Separate Stable

Garages and stables, particularly old ones that are inclined to generous size, are often used by artists for their studios. The buildings are completely separate from the main house, so they are private and quiet, and the second-level loft space offers much headroom. The farm outbuilding shown below, before and after remodeling, demonstrates how a stale, under-roof storage area was turned into productive and handsome living-working space for an artist-illustrator. Roger Pellaton, Architect.

Above right. Gable-end windows provide a view and abundant light for a secondary drawing area in the refurbished loft. The many-drawered chest next to the artist's table stores brushes, paints, and paper. It was originally a carpenter's tool chest.

Below right. The adjacent attic corner contains reference books, a table for slide viewing, and a collection of American political memorabilia mostly from the nineteenth century. Antique toys are another favorite of the artist. The two men on the windmill-weather vane, in the foreground, saw logs as fast as the wind blows.

Above. The primary work center for the artist-illustrator overlooks a new deck extension reached through a sliding glass door. The stairway leads to a private entrance at the ground level next to the garage doors. A pegboard divider at the head of the stairs shields the work area from the entry and displays more of the owner's collections.

Left. This is the shape of the original structure before any remodeling was done.

Theatrical Interior

The country home of a New York stage designer is the scene of this workroom addition. The new one-room space is L-shaped, with a 16'/5m ceiling height at the roof ridge. This theatrical interior volume is dominated by a cathedral window that faces north for constant light. Bruce P. Helmes, Architect.

Above. The studio, basically contemporary in shape, is clad in yellow clapboard to match the three-story, 150-year-old house and the connecting link. Privacy for the new space is assured by its cul-de-sac location. The gable-high, small-paned window is a combination of a colonial design in a bold, modern outline.

Below. Every corner of the work area of the L-shaped studio is flooded with constant light from the north and large expanses of white wall amplify the light throughout the room. As a supplement to daylight, spotlights mounted on electrified ceiling tracks can be moved to any position along the track and tilted to the angle desired.

Opposite page. The sitting area of the studio centers around the ten-foot-wide fireplace built of native field stone. The mantel-lintel set in the stone is an old wood beam. For a provincial look the ceiling is surfaced with rough-sawn cedar and the flooring is terra cotta quarry tile—both played against walls of white.

11. Country Kitchens

Almost all modern American homemakers approve of and welcome the mechanized magic of our time- and labor-saving, space-age kitchen equipment. But the sterile design approach to the room that contained these modern wonders was too barren and forbidding. The efficient laboratory look was not wanted in the most-used room in the house—the vast majority of American families eat all their meals in the kitchen, and in many homes it is the primary daytime living space.

As a reaction to such a clinical approach, the country kitchen has found great vogue as a design scheme that easily assimilates the new apparatus and, at the same time, extends a homelike atmosphere to a center of family activity. The country kitchen has a provincial or colonial character that calls for the use of rustic materials such as handhewn beams, natural wood paneling and cabinetry, brick, clay tile, stone, copper, pewter, brass, and iron.

Compact and Country Practical

Hand-painted clay tiles, bevel-edged wood paneling, and countertops of vertical-grain hard maple compose a provincial backdrop for this east-end Long Island, New York kitchen (opposite). Its tiny U-shape is most efficient for the one-cook kitchen. Storage on the open shelves is within quick reach, and the absence of doors prevents head banging in a small space. There are many iron cooking pans and pots made of clay and copper, and in the foreground is an example of early American cooperage—a staved and hooped bowl for fruit. Tina Fredericks, Designer.

Photography note. Photographing kitchens can easily be an all-day affair depending on the amount of preparation necessary. Most of the work-a-day kitchen paraphernalia does not photograph well, so the decks must be cleared and a composition created piece by piece of the handsomest bowls, china, silver, napery, and cooking vessels available. Fresh fruit, flowers, and vegetables are all good accents. Supplemental lighting is almost always necessary—for these photographs, two 1,000 watt quartz lamps—and may need to be moved about to avoid the harsh glare from chrome-plated metal surfaces.

Kitchen Austrian

Opposite page. The owner of this kitchen in the New York suburbs got her inspiration for remodeling from a trip to the Austrian countryside. Originally, the 40'/12.2m long space was divided into five cubicles but the partitions were removed to make one continuous space that incorporated the kitchen work area and the dining room. "Distressed" wood beams, pine-paneled appliances and cabinets, and countertops, and backsplashes of handmade tile decorate the work center. Over the refrigerator, red clay drain pipes store wine. Janine Jordan Newlin, Designer.

Above. There is breakfast service for four on the peninsula counter opposite the sink. The right-angle counter divides the work area from the dining space. A rough-finish plaster antiques the ceiling and the resilient flooring has a flat-brick basketweave pattern.

Below. An old-world character pervades the dining area where the woods wear a soft patina of long use. The chandelier, accessories, pewter, and paintings were carefully chosen to fit the country scheme.

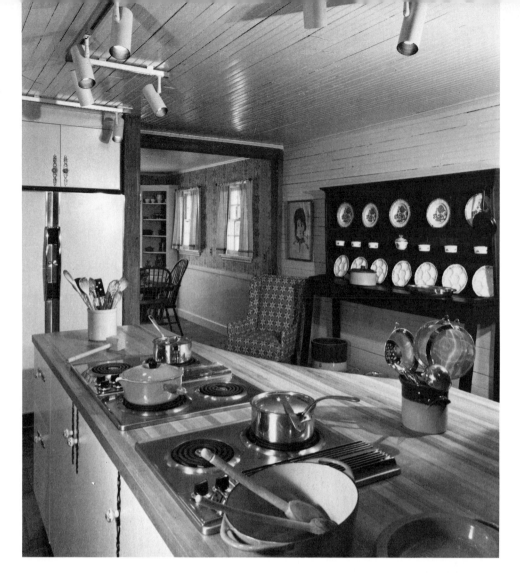

Saving the Best of the Old

Above. Country and contemporary combine in a Connecticut farmhouse kitchen. The owners couldn't bear to tear out every vestige of the original structure for the sake of modern convenience, so they kept the wide-open space and the narrow, bead-edge boards that cover the walls and ceiling. A few of the old framing timbers mark the entry to the dining room.

Below. In the breakfast room colonial table and chairs, corner cupboards, and wainscoting preserve the country charm. Large tiles of clay with random accent insets make up the floor surface for both of the rooms. Design is by Kitchens by Girard.

Provincial Modern

Opposite page. The simplicity of form and the use of natural materials inherent in provincial interiors is not at all incompatible with contemporary design theory. This country kitchen is thoroughly at home in a contemporary house. The entire cooking wall is built of used brick and contains a barbecue and electric cooktop with a ventilating hood and fan above. Pots and pans hang all in a row from the thick wood cornice above. The pass-through counter is of polished slate. George van Geldern, Architect.

Up to Date in a Barn Setting

Opposite page. 150-year-old structural timbers set the country motif for a New Jersey kitchen in a remodeled barn. To carry out the provincial theme, the cabinets are made of stained pine with wrought-iron strap hinges; paint-wiped brick covers the wall surfaces; and provincial kitchen tools and utensils are everywhere. Unobtrusive lighting over the work area is effected by recessing fluorescent light tubes behind translucent plastic sheets between the ceiling joists. William M. Thompson, Architect.

Collector's Kitchen

Above. The breakfast area in the kitchen of a new New England colonial house is a faithful reproduction of its 200-year-old ancestors. Antique paneling, beams, mantelpiece, flooring, and wainscoting were all parts of doomed, two-century-old houses that were painstakingly collected, refinished and installed with meticulous attention to detail. Architect: Norris Fremont Prentice

12. Crow's Nests

Solitaire, in addition to being a card game, is also defined as "a gem set alone"—an apt description for the hideaway rooms and spaces shown in this chapter. Everyone needs periods of solitude . . . times for reflection, reassessment, contemplation. A private retreat as part of a house provides such space for tranquility. The architects who designed the solitary spots illustrated here chose locations that were removed from the noise and activity of daily living. They particularly sought elevation to stimulate perspective and inspiration.

Angles in Space

An aerie on the top floor of a three-story contemporary house (opposite) has a lookout to the horizon. The architect designed the house in a vertical form in order to get an unobstructed view over the surrounding forest that would encompass the Hudson River Valley and the foothills of the Catskill Mountains to the west. This place of retirement is the deck off the master bedroom. The sharply angled planes of the railing and eave edge carry the eye into open space. The adjoining bedroom appears on the next page. Frank Edward Dushin, Architect.

Photography note. Photographing hideaways is one of the more strenuous aspects of architectural photography, since these nooks and niches are usually located in out-of-the way places at the top of many stairs. When using a view camera on a tripod, everything that will be needed should be taken for one trip. The light meter, film packs, and filters can be put in a small bag. An extreme wide-angle lens and one light stand are usually appropriate for small spaces.

Below. A sliding glass door opens the master bedroom to the deck. Frameless panels of sliding glass face the entire length of the west wall of the room. Note the transparency achieved by the delicate glass-to-glass corner in the foreground. The commanding 180- degree-aspect from the room creates the feeling of being on a ship's bridge. The chimney breast over the fireplace has a white stucco finish with insets of native stone.

Ranger Station

Above. Tree house interior is one large room screened on four sides for view, light, and ventilation. The massiveness of the roof structure contrasts with the airy openness of the wall-less space. Don Reiman, Architect.

Left. There is no ambiguity about the intentions of this tree house building. No casual traffic transgresses here from either house or garden. A narrow walkway connects the screened outdoor room with a deck that spans the rear of the main house. The second-story height captures the view as well as insuring privacy.

Urban Backyard

Right. Seclusion in the city was found on the rooftop of a living room addition to the rear of a Manhattan townhouse. The old brick walls of the original structure bordering the new roof terrace were painted white to reflect the sun's rays into the living area. Pepper and tomato plants, grown in grocery boxes, are part of the landscaping. Clay drain tiles are used to cap the wall edges.

Below. A circular steel staircase connects the ground-level terrace with the roof garden. Mats of woven reeds are tied to a security fence facing a neighbor's yard to block the view. Stephen B. Jacobs, Architect.

Roof-high Seclusion

Above. While planning the expansion of a small suburban house outside of New York City, the architect and owners found space for this hideaway-sewing room. It is located at the very top of the new two-story living area and has a tree-top view through the glass gable-end at the back of the house. A factory-made circular staircase is the only access to the nook from the living room below. The height of the space gives it a welcome isolation. George van Geldern, Architect.

Snow Country Retreat

Above. A sky-high bunkroom in a Vermont ski house is a quiet refuge several floors above the activity areas below. The tiny room has everything built in to save floor space. The lower level of the platform consists of a sitting surface for dressing and a giant storage chest with a hinged top. The middle stage has open-shelf storage for often-used items. At window level, the bunk bed has a panorama of prevailing snow conditions. John Hausner, Architect.

Sea View Seclusion

Opposite page. A small, private deck on the second level of a beach house in eastern Long Island has a view of the Atlantic beyond the dunes in the background. The framework of the house proper extends to nominally enclose the outdoor space making the deck seem like a room. Architectural definition of outdoor space creates a feeling of intimacy and human scale that makes it attractive. Robert L. Rotner, Architect.

13. Green Rooms

Bringing the outdoors in is a strong trend in residential design and one that shows no sign of abating. Every year we see new and inventive ways of opening interior spaces to more sunlight, with broad walls of glass, giant skylights, and even room-size greenhouses that are part of the floor plan.

Paralleling the expanding use of glass has been the great plant invasion. Almost every house and apartment has its indoor garden somewhere. It seems the more urban the setting the higher the concentration of flora. There are hanging plants, planting beds, planting troughs, carts on wheels that follow the sun, trees in pots (with and without wheels), terrariums, plant tanks, showcase racks, roof-top and courtyard gardens, window greenhouses, and full-size greenhouses equipped with temperature, humidity, and shade controls.

All four of the garden rooms shown here were recently built (three of the four are house additions) and hence reflect the liveliness of the movement to the greening of the indoors.

Plants are Part of the Plan

Plants thrive in a new garden room (opposite) at the back of a suburban builder house. The room was designed for optimum growing conditions with a southern exposure of sliding glass and overhead skylights. The loft space provided by the angled roof plane makes a decorative, well-lighted receptacle for displaying plants. F. Lincoln Geiffert, Architect.

Photography note. Strong sunlight is a major problem in photographing rooms with large areas of glass. If the exposure is set for the light intensity at the window, the rest of the room will be underexposed. A reading taken away from the window, where it is darker, will render the glass area white from overexposure. To achieve as close a balance as possible between window and room illumination, one can wait for the sun to move to the other side of the house or add sufficient artificial light indoors with floodlight and flash. In some cases translucent shades and draperies may be closed and will not detract from the rendition of the window design.

Flora in the Foyer

Opposite page. A lush growth of greenery greets visitors to a contemporary house on eastern Long Island where skylights span the entire width of a brick-paved entry foyer. Hanging plants are suspended from the roof rafters that frame the skylight panels. In the foreground is a gravel-bed planter with pots of sunflowers. The brick runway extends to the dining area. Eugene Futterman, Architect.

Greenhouse Addition

Above. A lean-to greenhouse addition was the answer to a New England couple's need for a place to pursue their gardening hobby. The work center is an integral part of the floor plan. It is situated in an L-shaped corner in the back of the house and opens to the living room, left, the terrace, rear, and the family room in the foreground. Automatic controls maintain the temperature and humidity at ideal levels.

Tropical Interior

Below. An informal room that was light and airy and conducive to growing things was what was missing from this home in upstate New York. The profusion of plants and the sunny atmosphere have a magnetic attraction to family and visitors alike. The room has become a center for group activities, hobbies, and school projects. On clear winter days the warm, plant-filled interior seems almost tropical. A breakfast area occupies a corner in the background under the dropped ceiling. A wood-slat shade rolls down from the roof beam to intercept the sun on particularly hot days. Bruce P. Helmes, Architect.

14. Indoor Pools

The advent of the indoor swimming pool on the American residential scene is a recent occurrence. Previously, the indoor pool had belonged only to the very rich and could be seen, with some difficulty, enclosed in huge glass pavilions or conservatories.

The first attempts at indoor pool design, in the current trend, were depressing failures. This was probably because the pool room was looked upon as any other room, except that it would present great moisture-control problems. The resulting interiors surrounding the pools were damp, dark, and airless.

As more architects became interested in this aspect of residential design, the essential quality indispensable to the indoor pool was realized—it must be as much like an outdoor pool as possible. The single element most important to the pool environment is the sun. Sunlight should saturate the pool area through skylights and walls of glass, and there should be views to the outside landscape as well as planting inside. Doors and windows should open to admit fresh air in the warm weather. When the pool is closed to the outdoors, automatic controls monitor the air distribution, temperature, and humidity.

Light, Space and Water

A great body of water in an architectural composition must have proportionate amounts of other natural elements surrounding it. The most important are light and space. The proper esthetic balance is achieved in this indoor pool addition (opposite) to a house overlooking the Hudson River in New York State. LeRoy van Lent, Architect.

Photography note. Indoor pools are best photographed on clear days when the play of light on the surface of the water can be captured. A high camera level and lowered lens position will see the most water area. When the water is in motion, the surface will have texture.

Above. The pool enclosure is open on three sides to a view of the Hudson Valley. When the weather permits, the sliding glass doors open to the fresh air. Panels of fixed glass add light and view to the interior. The roof trusses are boxed in plywood with triangular cut-outs emphasizing the structural enclosure.

Below. Comforts are provided by a sitting area at the edge of the pool. Tufted carpeting is warm and dry underfoot, and furniture is made of woven wicker in a natural finish.

Opposite page. A skylight of clear plastic panels crowns the pool area. Glistening rectangles of sunlight play across the textured surface of the water. A railinged balcony and staircase connect the main body of the house with the pool.

A New Room of Water

Opposite page. An immense skylight of translucent plastic panels bathes this luxurious indoor pool in warmth and brightness. The ceiling structure is composed of 3″/75mm-thick white spruce planking supported by cross beams of laminated Douglas fir—the wood surfaces are bleached, stained, and wiped to a subtle white patina. Hand-made Italian tiles, 3/4″/20mm thick, decorate the walls; pool walls are in a mosaic pattern.

Above. At one end of the 41′/12.2m-long pool room is the sitting area carpeted in an indoor-outdoor shag wall-to-wall carpet. Large potted plants bring the outdoors in. The open door leads to a dressing room; next to it is the sauna. An exercise table, electrically heated towel rack, and television are useful accessories.

Below. The pool addition extends at a right angle from the rear of the house. While the original house is traditional in design, the pool structure is contemporary, but the two are harmoniously related by the matching of building materials on the exterior of the pool house. LeRoy van Lent, Architect.

185

The Great Indoors

Above. It is hard to conceive that an indoor pool could be any more "outside" than this one. The setting for the water is completely natural. Space flows through the glass enclosure as far as the eye can see, making the pool a part of the landscape. During the warm months of the year fresh air flows into the interior through openings provided by the sliding glass doors and the sliding windows above. The green of the surrounding woods is continued indoors with potted plants and trees set in dirt cavities in the flagstone terrace. George van Geldern, Architect.

Opposite page. The sandwich-panel sunroof appears as a weightless plane of light across the pool room. A bench seat extends the length of the deck that bridges the space between the grounds and the pool. A part of the bedroom wing of the house appears at left of the photo.

Picture Credits

House & Garden Guides, © 1962, 1964–1976, Condé Nast Publications, Inc., pages 31–45, 72–99, 116–123, 141, 147, 158–161, 165, 168–171, 173, 175–185.

New Homes Guide, Holt, Rinehart and Winston, Inc., 1969–1971, pages 17–29, 138, 145, 151, 172.

Home Modernizing Guide, Holt Rinehart and Winston, Inc., 1969–1971, pages 110–112, 128–135, 142–144, 152–153, 174.

House Beautiful's Special Publications, Division of the Hearst Corporation, pages 54–59, 60–71, 106–109, 113–115, 124, 144, 148–150, 156–157, 163.

House plans drawn by George J. Gaspar

Index

Edited by Connie Buckley
Designed by James Craig
Set in 12 point Bodoni Book by Gerard Associates/Graphic Arts, Inc.
Printed by Halliday Lithographic Corp.
Bound by A. Horowitz and Sons